DESKTOP PUBLISHING ACTIVITIES

Manual

Iris Blanc
Totenville High School
Staten Island, New York

Contributing Editor:

Elaine Langlois

JOIN US ON THE INTERNET
WWW: http://www.thomson.com
EMAIL: findit@kiosk.thomson.com   A service of I(T)P®

South-Western Educational Publishing
an International Thomson Publishing company I(T)P®

Cincinnati • Albany, NY • Belmont, CA • Bonn • Boston • Detroit • Johannesburg • London • Madrid
Melbourne • Mexico City • New York • Paris • Singapore • Tokyo • Toronto • Washington

ISBN: 0-538-67793-7

5 6 7 8 MZ 04 03 02 01 00 99

Printed in the United States of America

ITP®
International Thomson Publishing

South-Western Educational Publishing is a division of International Thomson Publishing,
Inc. The ITP logo is a registered trademark used herein under license by South-Western
Educational Publishing.

CONTENTS

PREFACE iv

WARRANTY AND HOTLINE INFORMATION viii

TEACHING NOTES ON EXERCISES 1-110 1

SOLUTIONS TO ON-YOUR-OWN PROJECTS 119

SOLUTIONS TO SIMULATION ACTIVITY 124

TEACHING NOTES ON APPENDIX A 133

PREFACE

DESKTOP PUBLISHING ACTIVITIES introduces students to the newest and most commonly used features of desktop publishing software through skill-building exercises. This text, which can be used with any desktop publishing software in Windows or Macintosh format, provides 110 hands-on, step-by-step exercises that students can complete with a minimum of instruction to create workplace and personal documents such as letters, letterheads, logos, memos, reports, forms, resumes, invitations, announcements, flyers, news releases, advertisements, agendas/conference programs, menus, brochures, newsletters, presentation graphics, and documents formatted for Internet publication. Fifteen *On-Your-Own Projects* allow students to apply the skills they have learned to create their own documents. A capstone simulation activity places the student in a realistic business setting as the Publications Assistant to the busy director of a city tourism bureau.

After completing the exercises in this text, students will be able to:

■ Apply generic desktop publishing concepts through sequential exercises and applications.

■ Manipulate desktop publishing software to enhance and create documents appropriate for a business environment or for personal use.

All exercises in the text (and the text itself) were created using PageMaker 6.0 for Windows and an IBM-compatible PC. Many exercises were designed by professional graphic design consultants on the desktop, expressly for DESKTOP PUBLISHING ACTIVITIES.

This text does not focus on design concepts, but rather on using desktop publishing as a tool for creating and enhancing documents. The text provides sample document formats, general guidelines for design, and design pointers specific to the project at hand. While creating desktop layouts does require some design skill, this book gives the non-designer the information and background needed for document design. Students will be surprised at how quickly they are producing professional-looking desktop-published documents on their own.

Role of This Text in the Curriculum

DESKTOP PUBLISHING ACTIVITIES is appropriate for use in post-secondary and high school classes in computer applications, business computer applications, office technology, and word processing—any course in which computers with Windows 95 or Macintosh capabilities are used. The text provides ample material for a one-semester course in desktop publishing. Estimated completion time is 35 to 120 hours.

Students will derive the most benefit from using DESKTOP PUBLISHING ACTIVITIES if they have a basic background in computer use (e.g., if they are comfortable using a mouse and common program features like menus and dialog boxes). Appendix A provides optional exercises in such basic computer concepts. Some familiarity with word processing is also desirable.

Organization of the Text

The text is organized into two parts. Part I, *Introduction to Desktop Publishing*, focuses on the introduction and development of desktop publishing skills in 60 hands-on, step-by-step exercises. This part uses a sequential, building-block approach, focusing on skill development. The exercises are grouped into seven lessons on topics such as formatting text, working with imported text and graphics, and using special effects and features.

In Part II, *Creating Presentation Documents*, the focus shifts to document production. In 50 exercises, students produce 18 types of documents in attractive and sophisticated desktop-published formats. These exercises are grouped into 14 lessons on the basis of type of document produced. They are followed by 15 *On-Your-Own Projects*, in which students apply their desktop publishing and design skills to create their own documents with a minimum of direction. The text concludes with a capstone simulation activity, eight jobs in which students take the part of Publications Assistant to the busy Director of Communications of a city visitors bureau, designing and producing a variety of documents to promote tourism.

The exercises in DESKTOP PUBLISHING ACTIVITIES are presented in a format designed to be easy for students to work with and efficient for instructors to use in presenting lesson concepts and assessing work. In most cases, *Concepts* and *Instructions* appear on the left page of a two-page spread; a sample solution appears on the right page. Students thus have at hand, without having to turn pages or flip through the book, all the information they need to complete an exercise as well as a model towards which to work.

The organization of each exercise is as follows:

Learning Objectives	The *Learning Objectives* set forth the skills that are the focus of the exercise.
Terms (Part I only)	Terms discussed and defined in the exercise are listed in the *Terms* section.
Desktop Techniques Applied (Part II only)	This section lists the desktop publishing techniques highlighted in the exercise.
Concepts	The *Concepts* section discusses concepts introduced in the exercise. This section appears in most exercises in Part I and some exercises in Part II.
Instructions	The *Instructions* section provides step-by-step directions for completing the exercise.
Exercise	For most exercises, the *Exercise* page shows the document as it should appear in final form. Students can use this page as a guideline when working; instructors can use it to assess student work.

The text includes these additional features:

- *Appendix A* provides optional exercises in basic computer skills such as using a mouse, working with menus and dialog boxes, and working with windows.

- A *Glossary* defines terms used throughout the text.

- A comprehensive Index is included.

Hardware and Software

To complete the applications in DESKTOP PUBLISHING ACTIVITIES, students will need a computer, a high-quality printer, and desktop publishing software. System requirements will vary depending on the software to be used. Check your software documentation for computer system requirements. The exercises were written using PageMaker 6.0 for Windows, but they are generic in nature and may be used with any desktop publishing software.

Many exercises in DESKTOP PUBLISHING ACTIVITIES require clip art. The clip art in the text is from the CLIP ART FOLIO: A LIBRARY OF DESKTOP PUBLISHING ART (South-Western Publishing Co.), available in both IBM and Macintosh formats. Any clip art available to students may be used, however.

Word processing, table, spreadsheet, graphics, and presentation graphics software are not required for DESKTOP PUBLISHING ACTIVITIES, but use of any of such programs will enhance the learning experience for students. Instructions for individual exercises specify when the optional use of such software would be appropriate. If a scanner is available, students could use it to scan photographs and other types of printed artwork to add to their publications.

Organization of the Teacher's Manual

This TEACHER'S MANUAL provides the following information for each exercise in the student text:

Lesson number

Exercise number

Disk Files	This section lists files from previous exercises ("data files"), files from the template disk ("template files"), and graphics files required to complete the exercise.
Learning Objectives	The *Learning Objectives* set forth the skills that are the focus of the exercise.
Terms	Terms discussed and defined in the exercise are listed in the *Terms* section.
Preparation/Materials	This section describes any preparation required beforehand, such as obtaining appropriate clip art or working through an exercise.
Teaching Suggestions	This section provides suggestions for presentation of the material.
Settings	Margin settings are listed here.
Solution	Since most solutions are displayed in the student text, this section usually consists of a description of the parameters of the solution; (e.g., the title should be in a 30-point bold sans serif font). Solutions not shown in the student text are displayed in the manual. Solutions for *On-Your-Own Projects* and the simulation activity appear in the manual. There are no solutions disks.

Transparency masters are provided for selected exercises.

Guidelines for Teaching

It is recommended that desktop publishing concepts and applications be taught using the developmental approach: apperception, motivation, introduction to new vocabulary concepts, teacher demonstration, application, and summaries.

The exercises in the text were created using PageMaker 6.0 for Windows and an IBM-compatible PC. Not all desktop publishing programs use all the features taught in the text. You may need to modify exercise steps or omit some exercises depending on the features of the software you are using.

Many exercises in DESKTOP PUBLISHING ACTIVITIES require clip art. The clip art used throughout the text is from the CLIP ART FOLIO: A LIBRARY OF DESKTOP PUBLISHING ART (South-Western Publishing Co.), available in both IBM and Macintosh formats. Any clip art available to students may be used, however. In this manual, the *Disk Files* and *Preparation/Materials* sections for each exercise describe the type of clip art the exercise requires so that you can have appropriate clip art available to students when they need it.

You will need to instruct students on where to save their data files and from what location to place their template and clip art files. We strongly recommend that you have students work from the hard drive. Saving to and placing files from the hard drive will speed desktop work considerably.

The Template Disk

The template disk provided with DESKTOP PUBLISHING ACTIVITIES contains 54 documents in the following formats:

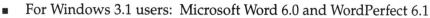

- For Windows 3.1 users: Microsoft Word 6.0 and WordPerfect 6.1
- For Windows 95 users: Microsoft Word 7.0
- For Macintosh users: Microsoft Word 6.0

Template disk files are provided for all but the shortest documents. (When students must key a short document, the exercise instructions direct them to do so.) Students do not work with these files in a word processor, but import them directly into their desktop publishing documents and format them there, as professional desktop publishers do. You may wish to have students key some documents, instead of using template disk files, to reinforce keying skills, particularly if they have access to a word processor.

Evaluation

Students should be evaluated on the basis of their performance of exercise objectives in the time specified and their ability to follow exercise instructions, not on their ability to design. It is recommended that you divide the number of steps required to complete an exercise into 100 to arrive at a point deduction on the exercise. The 15 *On-Your-Own Projects* and the eight jobs in the simulation activity should be subjectively evaluated on students' use of desktop publishing skills and basic design knowledge to produce an attractive document: A = very effective; B = effective; C = somewhat effective; D = not effective.

Electronic Media
Limited Warranty

South-Western Educational Publishing ("South-Western") extends the following warranty to only the original customer:

Warranty Coverage

This warranty covers the media on which the South-Western software/data are recorded. This limited warranty does not extend to the information contained on the media and in the accompanying book materials (the "Software/data"). The media product is warranted against malfunction due to defective materials or construction. This warranty is void if the media product is damaged by accident or unreasonable use, neglect, installation, improper service, or other causes not arising out of defects in material or construction.

Warranty Duration

The media product is warranted for a period of three months from the date of the original purchase by the customer.

Warranty Disclaimers

The following should be read and understood before purchasing and/or using the media:

a. Any implied warranties that arise out of this sale are limited in duration to the above three-month period. South-Western will not be liable for loss of use of the media or other incidental or consequential costs, expenses, or damages incurred by you, the consumer, or any other user. Furthermore, South-Western will not be liable for any claim of any kind whatsoever by any other party, against the user of the Software/data.

b. South-Western does not warrant that the Software/data and the media will be free from error or will meet the specific requirements of the consumer. You, the consumer, assume complete responsibility for any decisions made or actions taken based on information obtained using the Software/data.

c. Any statements made concerning the utility of the Software/data are not to be construed as expressed or implied warranties.

d. SOUTH-WESTERN MAKES NO WARRANTY, EITHER EXPRESSED OR IMPLIED, INCLUDING BUT NOT LIMITED TO ANY IMPLIED WARRANTY OR MER-CHANTABILITY AND FITNESS FOR A PARTICULAR PURPOSE, REGARDING THE SOFTWARE/DATA AND MAKES ALL SOFTWARE/DATA AVAILABLE SOLELY ON AN "AS IS" BASIS.

e. In no event will South-Western be liable to anyone for special collateral, incidental, or consequential damages in connection with or arising out of the purchase or use of the Software/data. The sole and exclusive liability of South-Western, regardless of the form of action, will not exceed the purchase price of the media.

f. Some states do not allow the exclusion or limitation of implied warranties or consequential damages, so the above limitations or exclusions may not apply to you in those states.

Further Disclaimers of Warranty

South-Western will extend no warranty where the software is used on a machine other than that designated on the software package.

Media Replacement

Provided that you, the customer, have satisfactorily completed and returned a copy of the License Agreement, South-Western will replace, during the warranty period, any defective media at no charge. At South-Western's option, the defective media must be returned, postage prepaid, along with proof of purchase date. Please contact South-Western at the address shown below for return instructions before returning any defective media.

South-Western Educational Publishing
Media Services
5101 Madison Road
Cincinnati, OH 45227

Legal Remedies

This warranty gives you specific legal rights, and you may also have other rights that vary from state to state.

Technical Support Hotline

The Technical Support Hotline (800/543-0453) is available to help you with any technical problems you may be having with this media product.

If you identify a problem, please check your hardware to make sure it is working properly. If the hardware is functioning correctly, call the number given. Please have the following information and materials with you when calling the hotline:

- program or template diskette
- text

- instructor's manual
- list of any error messages
- students' printouts
- description of the problem
- computer type and model
- computer's memory configuration
- version number of operating system
- name and version number of commercial software (if applicable)

Please do not permit your students access to the hotline number. If you want to order software, call (800) 354-9706. If you need product information, call (800) 824-5179.

LESSON 1: CREATING A NEW PUBLICATION

EXERCISE 1

DISK FILES: —

LEVEL: 1

LEARNING OBJECTIVES:

Start a new publication
Learn publication window features
Move around in a publication
Change the screen view
Close a document without saving
Exit from the software

TERMS: rulers, toolbox, icons, scroll bars, grabber hand, default

PREPARATION/MATERIALS:

- The text presumes that students have a basic familiarity with a mouse, windows, menus, and dialog boxes. Appendix A of the text (pages 239-242) provides exercises for students who need to practice these skills. You may wish to have such students complete the appropriate Appendix A exercises before doing Exercise 1.
- If a Help feature is not available, students may need access to the instruction manual provided with their software to complete the exercise.

TEACHING SUGGESTIONS:

- You may need to assist students in starting their desktop software and in starting a new document.
- If your software has a document setup dialog box, have students disregard it at this time and simply accept the defaults for this exercise. Document setup options will be discussed in Exercise 9.
- Identify each feature of your software's publication window. Show students how to move from page to page and how to move about on a page (e.g., scroll bars, grabber hand, and pointer and mouse button). Show students how they may see their position on the screen easily (e.g., cross hairs on the rulers or figures on a control palette).
- Explain the usefulness of being able to change screen views. Viewing the full screen, for example, is helpful in placing text and graphics. The actual size view is needed for keying and editing text. Demonstrate how to change views in your software (e.g., menu option, mouse, or zoom tool).
- If your software has a Help feature, examine it briefly with students.
- You may need to assist students in closing their document without saving it and exiting from the software.

SETTINGS:

Default.

SOLUTION:

Not applicable.

LESSON 1: CREATING A NEW PUBLICATION

EXERCISE 2

DISK FILES: —

LEVEL: 1

LEARNING OBJECTIVES:

Enter text
Save a publication

TERMS: text tool, I-beam, clicking an insertion point, text cursor, flush left

PREPARATION/MATERIALS:

In this exercise, students will create and save their first document. You will need to establish a place for them to save their data files. If they will save their data files on the hard drive, you may need to create, or have them create, a subdirectory or folder. If they will save their data files on a floppy disk, you will need to give them the disks.

TEACHING SUGGESTIONS:

- You may need to assist students in starting their desktop software and in starting a new document.
- If your software has a document setup dialog box, have students disregard it at this time and simply accept the defaults for this exercise. Document setup options will be discussed in Exercise 9.
- In the first few exercises, students key text in their desktop software, including longer documents that ordinarily would be keyed in a word processor. This procedure is intended to give them practice in keying text in the desktop program, to build their familiarity with basic program features, and to build upon any previous experience in word processing.
- Emphasize that all but the shortest documents should be created and edited in a word processor. Explain that word processors permit users to key and edit text much more rapidly and efficiently than desktop publishing software.
- Show students the text tool in their software and how to select it. Explain the conventions for entering text in your software.
- If your software has any tools for helping students place the text cursor properly (e.g., cross hairs on the rulers), demonstrate those tools.
- Instruct students in the conventions for naming files for their software. Tell them where files should be saved.
- You may need to assist students in closing their document and exiting from the software.

SETTINGS:

Default.

SOLUTION:

Not applicable. Students are not instructed to print their work until Exercise 5. If you do decide to have them submit a solution, note that text should begin 1″ from the top of the page and should match the text in the exercise. Of course, students should key the text line for line, except for the two longer paragraphs; for them, line endings may not match. Keying errors are acceptable at this point.

LESSON 1: CREATING A NEW PUBLICATION

EXERCISE 3

DISK FILES: —

LEVEL: -1

LEARNING OBJECTIVES:

Enter text
Save a publication

TEACHING SUGGESTIONS:

- This exercise allows students to practice entering text. Tell them not to attempt to format the letter. They will have an opportunity to add formatting in a later lesson. At that time, formatting a personal-business letter will be discussed. In addition, students will add a letterhead to the letter.

- Remind students that ordinarily this letter would be prepared in a word processor. They are keying it in their desktop publishing software for practice.

- You may need to review the procedure and location for saving documents.

- Direct students to retain all their data disk files. Many of the files will be used in subsequent lessons.

SETTINGS:

Default.

SOLUTION:

Not applicable. Students are not instructed to print their work until Exercise 5. If you do decide to have them submit a solution, note that text should begin 2" from the top of the page and should match the text in the exercise (line endings may not match, except of course for the short letter-part lines). Keying errors are acceptable at this point.

LESSON 1: CREATING A NEW PUBLICATION

EXERCISE 4

DISK FILES: —

LEVEL: -1

LEARNING OBJECTIVES:

Enter text
Save two versions of a publication

TEACHING SUGGESTIONS:

- This exercise allows students to practice entering text. They will format this type sampler in a later lesson.

- Students will use the save as command to save two versions of the document. Review the use of this command to save copies or different versions of a publication.

- Remind students to press Enter/Return only at the end of paragraphs. Reemphasize that their line endings may not match those in the exercise copy.

- Remind students to save their work periodically to avoid lost data.

- Remind students to retain all their data disk files. Many of the files will be used in subsequent lessons.

SETTINGS:

Default.

SOLUTION:

Not applicable. Students are not instructed to print their work until Exercise 5. If you do decide to have them submit a solution, note that text should begin 1" from the top of the page and should match the text in the exercise (line endings may not match, however). Keying errors are acceptable at this point.

LESSON 1: CREATING A NEW PUBLICATION

EXERCISE 5

DISK FILES: —

LEVEL: 1

LEARNING OBJECTIVES:

Enter text
Print a document

TERMS: resolution, service bureau, portrait orientation, landscape orientation

TEACHING SUGGESTIONS:

- Make sure students understand that **resolution** means the print quality of the final document. Printer resolution is measured in dots per inch. The more dots per inch a printer can produce, the better the quality of the printed document. Lasers for home and office use generally have resolutions of 300 to 600 dots per inch (dpi).

- Explain that most desktop-published documents will eventually be printed in large quantities. The user produces a master copy on a laser printer, which is then given to a print or photocopy shop for mass production on quality paper. Alternatively, users can give their document on disk to a service bureau for output on a high-quality laser. Users need to check first with the service bureau to discuss compatibility issues.

- Discuss printing options for your software. Identify the target printer for students. Make sure students understand portrait and landscape orientation.

- Direct students to save their files before printing, so that, if a problem should arise during the printing process, the file will be intact.

SETTINGS:

Default.

SOLUTION:

As shown in the exercise (the complete document, not the first saved portion). Text should begin 1" from the top of the page and should match the text in the exercise (line endings may not match, however). Keying errors are acceptable at this point.

LESSON 1: CREATING A NEW PUBLICATION

EXERCISE 6

DISK FILES: —

LEVEL: 1

LEARNING OBJECTIVES:

> Understand stories
> Understand text blocks
> Enter text in separate stories
> Print documents

TERMS: story, text block, windowshades, windowshade handles

PREPARATION/MATERIALS:

> Have available a few books, magazines, or newspapers for individual students or groups of
> students to examine.

TEACHING SUGGESTIONS:

- Make sure students understand the difference between stories and text blocks. A story is a
  single unit of text. It may be as small as one letter or as large as a multi-page publication. A
  story appears in a document in one or more text blocks. The reason for text blocks is so that
  text can be moved, made wider, made narrower, and otherwise manipulated to fit a
  document layout.

- Explain that keying separate stories is useful when you want different elements of text to be
  treated discretely. Highlight the example in the text. Have students look through books,
  magazines, or other publications and identify likely separate stories.

- Demonstrate selecting a text block with the pointer tool. Direct students to note the lines and
  handles. Discuss the purpose of the side handles (to make a text block narrower or wider).
  Explain the significance of an empty top or bottom handle, a top or bottom handle with a
  plus sign (there is more of the story in another text block), and a handle with an arrow (some
  of the story is not displayed—the handle must be pulled down to reveal the rest of the story).
  Tell students that they will work with text blocks in later exercises.

- Demonstrate deselecting a text block.

- Demonstrate creating separate text stories.

SETTINGS:

> Default.

SOLUTIONS:

> As shown in the exercises. For Exercise 6A, where the text blocks are located does not matter.
> For Exercise 6B, the separate sections of text should begin at 1", 1.5", and 2.5" from the top of
> the page. For both exercises, the separate sections of text should be separate stories. Keying
> errors are acceptable at this point.

LESSON 1: CREATING A NEW PUBLICATION

EXERCISE 7

DISK FILES: —

LEVEL: -1

LEARNING OBJECTIVES:

> Enter text in separate stories
> Print documents

TEACHING SUGGESTION:

> This exercise and the next allow students to reinforce their skills in keying separate stories. In upcoming exercises, the text they key will be formatted into finished desktop-published documents.

SETTINGS:

> Default.

SOLUTION:

> As shown in the exercise. Where the text blocks are located does not matter. Of course, students should key the text line for line, and the separate sections of text should be separate stories. Keying errors are acceptable at this point.

LESSON 1: CREATING A NEW PUBLICATION

EXERCISE 8

DISK FILES: —

LEVEL: -1

LEARNING OBJECTIVES:

Enter text in separate stories
Print documents

TEACHING SUGGESTION:

This exercise allows students to reinforce their skills in keying separate stories. In an upcoming exercise, the text they key will be formatted into a finished desktop-published document.

SETTINGS:

Default.

SOLUTION:

As shown in the exercise. Where the text blocks are located does not matter. Of course, students should key the text line for line (except for the last section of text), and the separate sections of text should be separate stories. Keying errors are acceptable at this point.

EXERCISE 9

DISK FILES: —

LEVEL: 1

LEARNING OBJECTIVES:

> Change default options
> Learn about document setup
> Change document setup options

TERMS: page size, dimensions, target printer, double-sided, facing pages

PREPARATION/MATERIALS:

> If a Help feature is not available, students may need access to the instruction manual provided with their software to complete the exercise.

TEACHING SUGGESTIONS:

- Have students access the document setup dialog box in their software. Discuss the options, particularly any options in your software that differ from those covered in the text. If necessary, review portrait and landscape orientation (page 8 of the text).

- Make sure students understand that the target printer may not be the same as the printer used to print interim proofs of a document. Remind them that desktop publishers may take their files to a service bureau for final output. Similarly, it is not unusual for desktop publishers to produce a document one printer and do their final output on another.

- Expand upon the importance of selecting at the time of document setup the target printer you will use to print your final document. The publication will be composed for that printer, with its fonts and settings. Changing the target printer later in the process of producing a document can cause fonts to become unavailable, line endings to shift, and so forth.

- Explain that desktop publishers may choose a lower resolution while they are producing a document so that pages will print more quickly. Unlike the target printer, resolution can be changed with no untoward effects. Remind students that **resolution** means the print quality of the final document and is measured in dots per inch.

SETTINGS:

> Will vary.

SOLUTION:

> Not applicable.

LESSON 2: CHANGING THE APPEARANCE OF TEXT

EXERCISE 10

DISK FILES: —

LEVEL: 1

LEARNING OBJECTIVES+: Use typefaces

TERMS: typeface, serif, sans serif, script, font

TEACHING SUGGESTIONS:

- Define **typeface** as all the characters (uppercase and lowercase letters, numbers, and symbols) of a single type design. Have students examine the typefaces in the illustration on page 15. Explain that each typeface has its own personality. Emphasize the importance of choosing a typeface that matches the message of a publication. Have students brainstorm when they might use some of the typefaces in the illustration.

- Make sure students understand the distinction between serif and sans serif typefaces. Point out that the first column of the illustration contains serif typefaces; the second, sans serif typefaces; and the third, script and symbol typefaces.

- Explain that serif typefaces are considered easier to read and are generally used for body text in publications such as magazines, reports, newspapers, and books. Sans serif typefaces are commonly used for headings. Script typefaces are sometimes used in announcements and invitations.

- Show students how to access type options in their software. If their software uses *font* for *typeface*, point that out. Make sure students understand the difference in publishing terminology between fonts and typefaces.

- Emphasize that desktop publishers usually use only two or three typefaces in a document. Using too many typefaces is sometimes called "the ransom note effect." Using just a few typefaces gives a publication an appearance of unity, consistency, and clarity. To achieve some variation in a document, desktop publishers can change the type size and type style of different elements: making headlines larger and bold, for example.

- You may wish to go over the exercise to be sure students understand what they are to do, particularly in Step 3. Note that Step 6 calls for the remainder of the exercise to be completed in groups. Whether you have students form groups or not, follow the exercise with a discussion of some of the typeface choices students have made and their reasons for them. As a class, decide on some of the best choices.

SETTINGS:

Default.

SOLUTIONS:

Students should submit a sheet of paper listing each typeface available in their software; the name of each typeface should be keyed in that typeface. For a symbol typeface, students should have keyed a few symbols and then keyed the name in a separate typeface. Next to the name of each typeface, students should have written whether it is a serif, sans serif, script, or decorative typeface. You may also wish to have students submit the lists of publications, chosen typefaces, and rationales they completed in Steps 7 and 8 of the exercise.

LESSON 2: CHANGING THE APPEARANCE OF TEXT

EXERCISE 11

DISK FILES: RESUME (data file)

LEVEL: 1

LEARNING OBJECTIVES:

> Use type styles
> Open/recall a publication
> Select text with the text tool

TERMS: type style, Roman (normal, medium), retrieve (open, get, recall), select (block)

PREPARATION/MATERIALS:

> A transparency showing text in the different type styles available in your software would be useful. Instead of or in addition to a transparency, you might obtain some publications using different type styles.

TEACHING SUGGESTIONS:

> ■ Define **type style** as modification of typefaces to add emphasis or contrast. Show students how to access type styles in their software and what type styles are available. A transparency showing the different type styles available in your software would be useful. If you have brought publications showing different type styles, circulate them among the class.

> ■ Emphasize that type styles should be used sparingly and for good effect. Go over the guidelines presented in the Concepts for using bold and italic type.

> ■ Explain how to open a file in your software and what term is used. Make sure students know how to navigate to the location where their data files are stored.

> ■ If necessary, demonstrate how to select text with the text tool. Students may have experience in selecting text from word processing and other computer applications.

> ■ The exercise uses just two type styles, bold and italic. For additional practice, you may wish to have students create a separate document in which they key the name of each type style available in their software and apply that type style to the name.

SETTINGS:

> Default.

SOLUTION:

> As shown in the exercise (line endings may vary). Students may choose any sans serif typeface (of course, it should be the *same* sans serif typeface throughout the publication). If you have students complete the last bulleted item above, they should also submit a separate document containing the name of each type style available in their software in that type style.

LESSON 2: CHANGING THE APPEARANCE OF TEXT

EXERCISE 12

DISK FILES: ELEMENT1 (data file)

LEVEL: 1

LEARNING OBJECTIVES:

Use different type sizes
Understand measurement options
Understand and change leading
Align text

TERMS: points, picas, leading

PREPARATION/MATERIALS:

Transparency 1, Measuring Type (page 13)
Transparency 2, Leading (page 14)

TEACHING SUGGESTIONS:

- Show Transparency 1. Explain how type is measured. Explain the terms *point* and *pica.*

- Show students how to access the measurement system option in their software. Examine the different measurement systems available. Tell students that, although desktop publishers work with picas, they will use the familiar inches system in this text.

- Demonstrate how to change the type size in classroom software. Have students note the different type sizes available. Refer students to the illustrations of type size in the exercise.

- Show Transparency 2. Explain how leading is measured. Emphasize that descenders are not included and that the measurement includes the size of the type. Type with 2 points between the lines is described as 10-point type on 12-point leading (10 + 2). It is written as 10/12 and expressed as "10 on 12."

- Explain that desktop publishing software sets the leading automatically at 120 percent of the point size of the type.   Demonstrate how to change the leading in classroom software.

- Help students realize the important role type size and leading play in readability. Go over the guidelines on page 18. Have students examine the four paragraphs at the bottom of Exercise 12 on page 19 and decide which type size/leading combination is most readable.

- Draw students' attention to the alignment options on page 18. Examine each option and when it is used. Show students how to access the alignment option in their software.

SETTINGS:

Default.

SOLUTION:

As shown in the exercise (line endings may vary). Typefaces and options may be different, depending on what is available in students' software.

Measuring Type

Type

Type is measured in points, from the top of the tallest letter to the lowest descending part of a letter.

Leading

Desktop Publishing

Baseline

Baseline

Leading is the vertical distance from the baseline of one line of text to the baseline on the following line. The text above is 60-point type on 72 points (1 inch) of leading.

EXERCISE 13

DISK FILES: ECOLOG (data file)

LEVEL: 1

LEARNING OBJECTIVES:

Change type size, type style, leading, and alignment
Create a letterhead
Learn personal-business letter format

TERMS: letterhead, personal-business letter, block format, open punctuation, mixed punctuation, enclosure/attachment notation

TEACHING SUGGESTIONS:

- Define **letterhead.** Introduce the **personal-business letter** and describe its use. Go through the formatting and letter parts, referring to the model on page 21 of the student text.

- Explain that, ordinarily, a personal-business letter would probably be prepared in a word processor unless it had a letterhead. Many simple letterheads can be created in word processors.

- Make sure students understand **block** format (all letter parts blocked at the left) and the difference between **open** and **mixed** punctuation. Open punctuation means no punctuation following the salutation or the complimentary close. Mixed punctuation means a colon follows the saluation and a comma follows the complimentary close.

SETTINGS:

Default.

SOLUTION:

As shown in the exercise (line endings may vary). The letterhead should be set just inside the default top margin. The text of the letter should begin 2 inches from the top of the page or may be centered vertically. Side margins should be at the software defaults. Students may choose any serif typeface for the body text and any sans serif typeface for the letterhead, but both typefaces should be 10-point and the body text leading should be 12-point. Errors in keying and end-of-line word division are acceptable at this point.

LESSON 2:   CHANGING THE APPEARANCE OF TEXT

EXERCISE 14

DISK FILES: RULES1 (data file)

LEVEL: 1

LEARNING OBJECTIVES:

Insert, delete, and replace text
Proofread work

PREPARATION/MATERIALS:

You may wish to provide rough and draft copy for students to proofread according to the guidelines in the Concepts on page 22.

TEACHING SUGGESTIONS:

- Show students how to insert, delete, and replace text in their desktop publishing software. If students have had previous word processing experience, draw comparisons between how they perform these tasks in their word processor and how they perform them in their desktop publishing software.

- Discuss the importance of producing accurate work. Go over the guidelines for proofreading discussed in the Concepts on page 22. You may wish to provide students with rough and draft copy to proofread. Students could proofread both individually and in pairs as described in the text.

- Go over the proofreader's marks illustrated on page 22.

SETTINGS:

Default.

SOLUTION:

As shown on page 17 (line endings may vary). Text should begin 1 inch from the top of the page.

EXERCISE 14

SOLUTION:

COMPUTER ROOM RULES AND REGULATIONS

All software in the computer center is copyrighted. Duplication of such material is strictly prohibited and illegal.

DO NOT

Bring outside software into the computer center.

Bring food and drinks into the classrooms at any time.

Smoke anywhere in the center.

Leave any scrap papers, printouts, etc., at your station.

Rearrange the hardware in the center without checking with your teacher.

Connect or disconnect plugs without your teacher's permission.

LESSON 2: CHANGING THE APPEARANCE OF TEXT

EXERCISE 15

DISK FILES: RESUME (data file)

LEVEL: 1

LEARNING OBJECTIVES:

Insert, delete, replace, and format text
Proofread work

TEACHING SUGGESTIONS:

This reinforcement exercise will give students practice in editing text.

SETTINGS:

Default.

SOLUTION:

As shown on the next page (line endings may vary). Text should begin 1 inch from the top of the page.

EXERCISE 15

SOLUTION:

James Constantino
43 Beacon Street
Amesbury, MA 01984-2234
(508) 555-8990

EDUCATION

A.A., Graphic Design, Glover College, 1997

High School Diploma, Amesbury High School, 1995

SCHOOL ACTIVITIES

Senior Designer, *Glover College Yearbook,* spring 1997. Worked with student committee to re-design the college yearbook on desktop publishing software.

Production Worker, *Glover Weekly News,* August 1996 to May 1997. Worked 15 hours a week designing pages and producing advertisements for college newspaper.

Dean's List, spring and fall 1996, spring 1997.

WORK EXPERIENCE

Publications Intern, Stearns and Socol Advertising, Boston, MA, fall 1996. Designed and produced flyers, newspaper advertisements, coupons, announcements, reports, and brochures.

Intern, Olivera Publishing, Salem, MA, spring 1997. Designed and produced technical manuals and sales catalog.

Volunteer, Glover Outreach Project, spring 1997. Worked Saturday afternoons doing repairs and light carpentry for low-income citizens.

REFERENCES

References available upon request.

LESSON 2: CHANGING THE APPEARANCE OF TEXT

EXERCISE 16

DISK FILES: ELEMENT (data file)

LEVEL: 1

LEARNING OBJECTIVES:

Cut, copy, and paste text

TERMS: cut, copy, paste, clipboard

TEACHING SUGGESTIONS:

- If students have had previous word processing experience, draw comparisons between how they cut, copy, and paste text in their word processor and how they perform these tasks in their desktop publishing software.

- Show students how to cut and copy text with the text tool. Demonstrate different selection methods in your software. If your software has a select all command, demonstrate that as well, preferably on a story that spans several text blocks. If necessary, review the concepts of stories and text blocks.

- If possible, open the clipboard and show students that cut or copied text appears there. Emphasize that cut or copied text remains in the clipboard and can be pasted again and again until something new is cut or copied to the clipboard. Make sure students understand that when the computer is turned off, the clipboard is emptied.

- Show students how to paste text with the text tool and the pointer tool. Explain that they must click an insertion point to insert text into existing text. To make the text a separate text block, they must either click outside existing text blocks or paste with the pointer tool selected.

- Make sure students understand the two instances in which they would use the pointer tool to select text to be moved or copied, at the bottom of the Concepts on page 25: (1) To move a text block into a different story, they would select the text block with the pointer tool, cut it, click an insertion point where they wanted the text, and paste it. (2) To move a text block physically, they would drag it. Demonstrate both exceptions. If your software has an option for dragging text straight horizontally or straight vertically (for example, pressing the Shift key while dragging), explain and demonstrate that option.

SETTINGS:

Default.

SOLUTION:

This exercise is for practice only. Students open the first document created in Exercise 5 and practice copying and moving text. Students are instructed to close the file without saving. If you want students to submit a solution, direct them to do so. Students' pages will vary widely.

LESSON 2: CHANGING THE APPEARANCE OF TEXT

EXERCISE 17

DISK FILES: RULES1 (data file)

LEVEL: 1

LEARNING OBJECTIVES:

Move the zero marker
Create a layout grid
Adjust the size of text blocks
Drag-place text
Turn off hyphenation

TERMS: grid, ruler guides, zero marker, drag-place

TEACHING SUGGESTIONS:

- Define a layout **grid** as an arrangement of non-printing guides that helps desktop publishers arrange text and graphics on a page. Show students what constitutes a grid in their software.

- If classroom software has ruler guides, demonstrate how to place, move, and remove them. If software has a snap-to option, demonstrate how to select it. If possible, place some text with the snap-to option selected so students can see its effect.

- If classroom software has a zero marker, identify it, and demonstrate how to reposition it. Explain that repositioning the zero marker is useful in many instances; for example, in measuring the distance between paragraphs of text and in placing ruler guides.

- Demonstrate how to widen and narrow a text block.

- Demonstrate how to drag-place text. Explain that drag-placing is useful for setting text in a precise area when you do not have column guides or margin guides to define the area.

- Show students how to turn off automatic hyphenation in their software. Proper word division will be discussed in a future exercise.

SETTINGS:

Default.

SOLUTION:

As shown in the text (line endings may vary). Note that the text and spacing in the student text example have been reduced to fit the example on the page. The type sizes and styles should be the same as those listed in the exercise. The title should appear just below the top margin; the rest of the text, just below the 2.5-inch horizontal ruler guide. The left and right boundaries for all the text are the vertical ruler guide at 4 inches from the right margin and the right margin. Text should not be hyphenated.

LESSON 2:   CHANGING THE APPEARANCE OF TEXT

EXERCISE 18

DISK FILES: RESUME (data file)

LEVEL: 1

LEARNING OBJECTIVES:

> Learn resume format
> Create a layout grid
> Cut, paste, and adjust text blocks
> Drag-place text
> Format text

TERMS: resume

PREPARATION/MATERIALS:

You may wish to provide samples of resumes in different formats for students to examine.

TEACHING SUGGESTIONS:

- Most students will be familiar with resumes. Emphasize that a resume often gives an employer a first impression of a student and can be the deciding factor in whether the student gets an interview. Resumes should be attractive, concise, informative, and error-free.

- If you have sample resumes to show students, circulate them, pointing out special features. The resume on page 29 has been designed for a recent graduate with little experience. Point out how using a generous top margin, setting the headings on the side, narrowing the body text width, and justifying the text makes the body of the resume look more full.

- Go through the required and optional sections of a resume, discussing the information that should be provided. Emphasize the importance of including dates. Information may be arranged from most important to least or from most recent back. The education section may include major, class standing, and relevant course work. For school activities, students should list each organization and describe their position. Work experience should include a description of the position, the name and location of the employer, and a brief description of the student's responsibilities.

- The activities in this exercise are essentially the same as those in Exercise 17. Go over any tasks you think require reinforcement (for example, drag-placing, repositioning the zero marker, or setting ruler guides). If a snap-to option is available on classroom software, remind students to choose it.

SETTINGS:

The top margin should be 1.5″; the rest of the margins should be 1″.

SOLUTION:

As shown in the text (line endings may vary). Note that the text and spacing in the student text example have been reduced to fit the example on the page. The type sizes and styles should be as shown in the exercise. The identifying information should appear just below the top margin. The headings should be right-aligned with the 1.5″ vertical guide. The body text should begin at the 2″ vertical guide. Four line returns should separate each major section. Body text should be fully justified, and text should not be hyphenated.

LESSON 2: CHANGING THE APPEARANCE OF TEXT

EXERCISE 19

DISK FILES: DESSERT, ECOLOG, ELEMENT1 (data files)

LEVEL: 1

LEARNING OBJECTIVES:

> Edit text with story editor
> Copy a publication

TERMS: story editor

TEACHING SUGGESTIONS:

- If your software has a story editor function, explain and demonstrate its use.

- Show students how to make a copy of a file in their software. Some programs have an option to open a copy of a file rather than the original. That option is preferable where available. Otherwise, students can open the document and save it immediately under a different filename using the save as command.

SETTINGS:

> Default.

SOLUTION:

> For **DESSERT1,** as shown on page 24. Where the text blocks are located does not matter. Students should have replaced two instances of "$1.00" with "$1.25" and two instances of "Cheesecake" with "Pie." Students will only submit copies of **ECOLOG** and **ELEMENT1** if they detected spelling errors in those documents. To review those documents, see pages 19 and 21 of the student text and pages 12 and 15 of this manual.

EXERCISE 19

SOLUTION:

COFFEE CUP
CAFE
Dessert
Menu

Coffee $1.25
Tea $1.25
Iced Tea $1.25
Iced Coffee $1.25
Espresso $1.25
Cappuccino $1.50
Iced Cappuccino $2.00
Cafe au Lait $1.10

$2.95
Blueberry Pie
Chocolate Torte
Ice Cream Sundaes
Fudge Fantasy Cake
Coffee Toffee
Pumpkin Pie
Great American Pie
Carrot Cake
Apple Pie
Lemon Squares
Brownies, Assorted Kinds
Fudge Fantasy
Chocolate Mousse Cake
Strawberries with Lemon Sorbet

LESSON 2: CHANGING THE APPEARANCE OF TEXT

EXERCISE 20

DISK FILES: RULES (data file)

LEVEL: 1

LEARNING OBJECTIVES:

Format text with the control palette

TERMS: control palette, character view, paragraph view, paragraph

TEACHING SUGGESTIONS:

- Make sure students understand the inconvenience involved in having to access several different commands to format the same text. Explain that they can use the control palette to change certain common attributes all at once for selected text.

- Show students how to display the control palette in classroom software. If the palette has two views, display each as you identify the palette features for changing attributes students have learned about so far in the text: typeface, type size, type style, leading, and paragraph alignment. Tell students the palette allows them to change other attributes, including graphics attributes, that they will learn about later in this text.

- Demonstrate how to make changes with the control palette. Show students that they can simply click an insertion point in a paragraph to change a paragraph attribute. Make sure students understand what **paragraph** means in desktop publishing software. Show students what happens when they make a control palette change with no text selected (the publication default is changed).

SETTINGS:

Default.

SOLUTION:

This is a practice exercise. Solutions will vary widely. The basic document appears on page 9 of the student text (the first saved version). The text should begin 1" down from the top of the page. The typeface, type style, type size, leading, and alignment of some of the text should have been changed. Students are told to close the file without saving.

LESSON 3: USING DRAWING TOOLS AND FILLS (SHADES)

EXERCISE 21

DISK FILES: —

LEVEL: 2

LEARNING OBJECTIVES:

> Create squares, rectangles, circles, ovals, and polygons
> Use fills (shades)
> Select, resize, move, and delete objects
> Change the stacking order

TERMS: drawing tools, crossbar, layering shapes

TEACHING SUGGESTIONS:

- A lot of information is presented in this first exercise. Subsequent exercises in this lesson will provide ample opportunity for reinforcement of concepts.

- Show students how to access the drawing tools in their software. Identify and demonstrate the use of each tool. If pressing a designated key while dragging constrains a rectangle to a square, a square to a circle, and so forth, demonstrate this procedure. If rounded corners is a menu option rather than a tool, show students where it is located.

- Show students how to select an object, including a transparent object like the circle at the top left on page 33 of the student text (they must click on an edge).

- Demonstrate how to resize an object in classroom software. If pressing a designated key while dragging causes an oval to become a circle, a rectangle to become a square, and so forth, demonstrate this procedure.

- Demonstrate how to delete an object.

- Demonstrate how to move an object. For a transparent object like the circle at the top left on page 33 of the student text, show students that they must drag by the edge (but not by a handle).

- Describe the fill options in your software. Make sure that students will understand what options to select for each of the objects they must create in Exercise 21.

- Demonstrate cutting, copying, and pasting objects.

- Make sure students understand layering and how to select underlying objects.

- For Exercise 21, you may need to direct students to draw different shapes or use different fills depending on the options available in classroom software.

SETTINGS:

The left margin should be .75"; the rest of the margins should be at the default setting.

SOLUTION:

As shown in the text. As discussed in the last bulleted item above, shapes and fills may vary depending on the options available in classroom software. Note that objects and spacing in the student text example have been reduced to fit the example on the page.

LESSON 3:   USING DRAWING TOOLS AND FILLS (SHADES)

EXERCISE 22

DISK FILES: SHAPES (data file)

LEVEL: 2

LEARNING OBJECTIVES:

> Draw lines (rules)
> Choose line sizes and patterns
> Edit drawn shapes
> Change a polygon to a star
> Use the power paste feature

TERMS: lines/rules, line tool, constrained-line tool, power paste, offset

TEACHING SUGGESTIONS:

- Demonstrate the line tools available in classroom software.

- Explore the line widths and designs available in classroom software.

- Show students how to select, delete, resize, move, and copy lines.   If pressing a designated key while dragging constrains a line drawn with the line tool to a 45-degree angle, demonstrate this procedure. If students must press a designated key to avoid distorting a line drawn with the constrained-line tool while resizing it, demonstrate this procedure.

- If classroom software has an option for changing a polygon to a star, demonstrate it.

- A power paste option, particularly with horizontal and vertical offset, will be extremely helpful in exercises such as this one and the next. If classroom software has this feature, demonstrate it.

SETTINGS:

Default.

SOLUTION:

As shown in the text. Exact placement and sizing are not important; the emphasis here is on being able to use the line tools and other drawing options to create objects. The star feature may not be available on all software. Borders may vary depending on the options available in classroom software. Note that objects and spacing in the student text example have been reduced to fit the example on the page.

LESSON 3:   USING DRAWING TOOLS AND FILLS (SHADES)

EXERCISE 23

DISK FILES: —

LEVEL: 2

LEARNING OBJECTIVES:

> Create objects with drawing tools
> Select multiple objects
> Work with grouped objects
> Align and distribute objects

TERMS: marquee, grouping objects, aligning objects, distributing objects

TEACHING SUGGESTIONS:

- Discuss the usefulness of being able to select more than one object at the same time.

- Demonstrate how to select multiple objects in classroom software. If drawing a marquee is one option in your software, show students how to do it, if possible. A marquee is difficult to imagine but easy to remember once students have seen it.

- Show students how multiple selected objects can be copied and moved.

- If classroom software has a grouping option, demonstrate its use. Show students how to resize a group. To resize a group proportionally, students may need to press a designated key (the Shift key, for example). Show students how to move and resize individual objects within the group. Explain how to "ungroup" objects.

- If classroom software has an align and distribute option, spend some time exploring its use. Have students draw several objects and experiment with the different align and distribute options.

SETTINGS:

Default.

SOLUTION:

As shown in the text. Exact placement and sizing are not important; the emphasis here is on being able to use the line tools and other drawing options to create objects. If classroom software does not have a grouping option that enables students to resize a group as a unit, students will not have a smaller copy of Object 3 as on page 37. Students are given a minimal amount of instruction in this exercise; for example, line widths, for the most part, are not given, and students are not told how to create the cigarette smoke. This exercise will help students develop their skills in using the drawing tools.

LESSON 3: USING DRAWING TOOLS AND FILLS (SHADES)

EXERCISE 24

DISK FILES: YARDFILL (data file)

LEVEL: 1+

LEARNING OBJECTIVES:

Create objects with drawing tools

TEACHING SUGGESTIONS:

■ Tell students that this exercise shows them how to create an attractive business letterhead using the drawing tools in their desktop publishing software.

SETTINGS:

All margins should be set at .75".

SOLUTION:

As shown in the text. Note that the text, objects, and spacing in the exercise have been reduced because of space constraints. All text should be in a sans serif typeface. The text "ardfill Nurseries" should be in 24-point bold. It should appear just inside the top margin and 2" from the left edge of the page. The address text should be 14-point and right-aligned. It should appear at the right margin and 1.5" down from the top of the page. The branches should be 8-point lines; the trunk should be a 12-point line. The foliage consists of circles with 20% fill and no border that should be of uniform size since students should have made one and copied it. Students' foliage patterns do not have to match the pattern in the exercise. The grass should consist of 2-point lines, none of which should be taller than 1". Again, students' grass does not have to match the grass in the exercise. The rectangle should have a solid fill and should be .5" tall. The rectangle should extend from the right margin to the left; it should be set at the bottom margin. The text "Peter Moss, Proprietor" should be in 14-point reverse and should appear in the center of the rectangle.

Since students draw some of the foliage above the top margin, it may be cut off during printing. In that contingency, students have been instructed to select everything at the top of the page, move it down, and print another copy. If they must do so, their "ardfill Nurseries" and address block text will be farther down than .75" and 1.5" respectively. If students have moved material down, they should have resized the tree trunk.

LESSON 3: USING DRAWING TOOLS AND FILLS (SHADES)

EXERCISE 25

DISK FILES: PAUL (data file)

LEVEL: 1+

LEARNING OBJECTIVES:

Create objects with drawing tools

PREPARATION/MATERIALS:

You may wish to provide sample invitations for students to examine.

TEACHING SUGGESTIONS:

- Discuss the use of invitations and how desktop publishing can be used to enhance an invitation. If you brought sample invitations, circulate them among the students.

SETTINGS:

The left margin should be 1"; the rest of the margins should be .75".

SOLUTION:

As shown in the text. Note that the text, objects, and spacing in the exercise have been reduced because of space constraints. All text should be in a sans serif typeface, center-aligned, and in the type sizes specified in the illustration on page 41 (the "5" should be 24-point reverse). Text blocks should be placed as indicated by the ruler guide markings in the illustration. The last text block should be set in 1" from the left and right. The cake should be centered. The cake plate should be approximately 5.25" wide by 1" tall. It should have a 2-point border; its inner ring should have a 1-point border. The cake is a rectangle with rounded corners, a 40% fill, and no border. The top of the cake is an oval with 20% fill and no border. The candles should be identical, since students should have created one and then copied it. The candles should consist of a rectangle 1/8" by .75" with a 1-point border and a paper fill. The wicks are 4-point lines. The flames may be ovals with hairline borders or stars as shown (in the illustration, a polygon was created and edited to a star). Students may use a different candle arrangement, if desired.

LESSON 3: USING DRAWING TOOLS AND FILLS (SHADES)

EXERCISE 26

DISK FILES: RULES1 (data file)

LEVEL: 2+

LEARNING OBJECTIVES:

Create objects with drawing tools

PREPARATION/MATERIALS:

You may wish to provide, or have students bring in, sample flyers.

TEACHING SUGGESTIONS:

- Discuss the use of flyers and how desktop publishing can be used to enhance a flyer. If you have sample flyers, circulate them among the students. Discuss the formatting features used and their effect.

SETTINGS:

The bottom margin should be .5"; the rest of the margins should be at the default setting.

SOLUTION:

As shown in the text; however, text will probably end far short of the bottom circle. The text, objects, and spacing in the exercise have been reduced because of space constraints. A dashed border, which will probably extend outside the margins, should surround the document. A 12-point line should appear just inside the dashed border at the top and should extend from the left to the right margins. Another 12-point line should appear at 2.25" and should extend from the right margin to be flush vertically with the text. A third 12-point line should appear along the bottom of the dashed box and should extend from the right margin to be flush vertically with the text. The four circles should have an 8-point line and should be distributed equally over a 7.75" vertical space with .25" between each pair of circles. Circles should be aligned vertically. Students are not given specific instructions on how to create the objects within the circles; they are expected to be able to examine the objects and determine how to create them. If they have a grouping option and the ability to resize grouped objects as a unit, students are told to copy and resize the cup and cigarette from Exercise 23. Each circle should have an 8-point diagonal line through it.

LESSON 4: WORKING WITH IMPORTED TEXT

EXERCISE 27

DISK FILES: FUN (template file)

LEVEL: 2+

PREPARATION/MATERIALS:

In this exercise, students will begin to work with the text files on the template disk. Text files have been provided in several popular word processing formats for students to import into their desktop publishing software. Before the class session, examine the manual for your desktop publishing software to determine what format students should use and whether they need to rename their template files (for example, append a special filename extension so the desktop publishing program will recognize the word-processed file). Decide also from what drive and directory or folder students will place their files. If students can copy their template files to the hard drive and place them from there, work will be faster.

In this text, students will not need to format files in their word processor for import into their desktop publishing software. All longer files are provided on the template and have already been formatted. If students do have a word processor, however, we recommend that you have them key selected files in their word processor instead of using the template file for practice. If you decide to have them do so, examine the manuals for your word processing and desktop publishing software to determine what formatting from the former the latter will accept. Instruct students on the conventions to use for formatting the file. For such exercises, direct students to format the file in their word processor to the extent their desktop publishing software will accept. Some general guidelines appear on page 44 of the student text.

LEARNING OBJECTIVES:

Import word-processed text

TEACHING SUGGESTIONS:

- Remind students that creating and editing text in a word processor is easier and more efficient than creating and editing it in desktop publishing software. Tell them that, from this point on, they will be importing longer text files from the template disk.
- Tell students what word processor format from the template disk to use. Tell them where their template files will be located. Tell them how to rename template files, if necessary. Emphasize that template files have already been formatted in the word processor for import.
- Go over the general guidelines on page 44 of the student text for formatting word-processed files. Alternatively, if students use a common word processor in class, go over the formatting guidelines for that word processor. If you do not plan to have students key and format any files in their word processor (see "Preparation/Materials," above), tell them so.
- Show students how to import text in their desktop publishing software. For software that has more than one text flow option (e.g., PageMaker), use manual text flow. Other text flow options will be discussed in Exercise 28.

SETTINGS:

The left and right margins should be 2". The top and bottom margins should be 1".

SOLUTION:

As shown in the text. Note that the text, objects, and spacing in the exercise have been reduced because of space constraints. Two 8-point lines will appear extending across the top and bottom margins from the left margin to the right. Text should be centered vertically between the lines. Body text should be in a serif typeface, 12/18, with hyphenation turned off. The title should be in sans serif 18-point bold and centered. Line endings may be different.

LESSON 4: WORKING WITH IMPORTED TEXT

EXERCISE 28

DISK FILES: PF (template file)

LEVEL: 2

LEARNING OBJECTIVES:

> Import word-processed text
> Create multiple columns
> Use text flow options
> Align text across columns

TERMS: gutter, automatic text flow, semiautomatic text flow, manual text flow, dummy text/*lorem ipsum*/copyfit file

TEACHING SUGGESTIONS:

- Show students how to set columns in their desktop publishing software. Identify the column borders and the gutter. If students have an option for creating custom columns, demonstrate that also. Emphasize that columns should be set in the desktop publishing software, not the word processor.

- If your software has different text flow options, demonstrate each option, and discuss when it would be appropriate. Automatic text flow is good for long publications when the text will flow straight onto pages and into columns. Tell students that, unlike the other options, automatic text flow automatically creates new pages as they are needed. Manual and semi-automatic text flow are good for short publications and when you want text to flow into only one column, not the other(s). Show students how semiautomatic text flow saves them the step of having to click on the plus sign in the bottom windowshade handle.

- Discuss the use of "dummy" text to experiment with a design.

- Show students how to set align text across columns as discussed on page 46 of the text.

- Suggest that students select the snap to guides option, if available, to help them place text.

SETTINGS:

Default.

SOLUTION:

As shown in the text. Note that the text, objects, and spacing in the exercise have been reduced because of space constraints. Text should be placed in two columns with the default software gutter. Text should be in a serif typeface, 12/18, and fully justified, with hyphenation off. The heading should be in 30-point bold, right-aligned, each word on a separate line, with hyphenation off. The word "USING" should appear 1.5" base to base from the top of the page. A 6-point line should appear 3" from the top of the page and should extend across the second column. A .5-point line should appear in the gutter, extending from the top to the bottom margin. Text should be aligned across columns.

LESSON 4: WORKING WITH IMPORTED TEXT

EXERCISE 29

DISK FILES: **PF** (template file)

LEVEL: 1

LEARNING OBJECTIVES:

Use different column layouts

TERMS: white space

PREPARATION/MATERIALS:

You may wish to provide, or have students bring in, samples of different types of documents with different numbers of columns.

TEACHING SUGGESTIONS:

- Discuss the number of columns students can set in their software. Go over the guidelines for numbers of columns in the text. If you or students have brought in sample publications, examine the different designs.

- Define **white space** and discuss its use in contributing to readability. Emphasize that number of columns, typeface, type size, alignment, white space, and rules must be considered together in contributing to the readability of a document.

SETTINGS:

Default.

SOLUTION:

Students should submit up to three copies of **PF1** in different column settings. The solutions submitted will represent what students consider their best efforts. Since solutions will vary so widely, no sample solution is provided. Consider choosing, yourself or with the class, the best examples, and discussing how each feature contributes to their effectiveness.

LESSON 4: WORKING WITH IMPORTED TEXT

EXERCISE 30

DISK FILES: **PF1** (data file)

LEVEL: 1

LEARNING OBJECTIVES:

> Divide words, lines, and paragraphs appropriately
> Use the hyphenation feature
> Use the widow/orphan feature

TERMS: hyphenation zone, widow, orphan

TEACHING SUGGESTIONS:

- Explain that, now that students are working with longer documents, issues such as hyphenation are becoming important. Go over the word division rules on page 49 of the student text. Emphasize that desktop publishers must often strike a balance between following the rules and making the text visually appealing.

- Demonstrate the hyphenation feature in classroom software.

- Demonstrate the widow/orphan feature in classroom software. Make sure students understand what widows and orphans are.

SETTINGS:

> Default.

SOLUTION:

> As shown on the next page. The solution has the same formatting as that for Exercise 28, except that hyphenation has been turned off, justification has been set to left, and widow/orphan protect has been activated. Students should have made good decisions on when to hyphenate and when not. Their line endings and hyphenation decisions may vary from those on the sample solution. Students may have deleted the final paragraph, as in the sample solution.

EXERCISE 30

SOLUTION:

USING PRACTICE TEXT

This is practice or "dummy" text that you can use for importing, placing, and playing purposes. Desktop publishers often use dummy text. When you are first designing a publication, you can flow a dummy text file in to see how your design will look with type. Desktop publishers also use dummy text for publications that will be produced periodically, such as a monthly newsletter. The dummy text serves as a placeholder for the different articles that will appear in each issue. You will learn more about using dummy text in this way in later exercises.

Some desktop publishing programs give you practice or "dummy" text that looks like Latin (but it's not). It is called a *lorem ipsum* file. Really, any file can serve as dummy text. The more it looks like the kind of text you will be using in your final publication, the better. You can manipulate and move sections of practice text as you desire. You can experiment with different elements such as typefaces, type styles, type sizes, and leading.

Later in this book, you will be given the opportunity to create your own projects. Before you tackle them, you will learn to plan your publication ahead by drawing a "thumbnail" sketch on a piece of blank paper. Drawing a thumbnail will give you direction in creating your page layout on the computer. The sketch should define the approximate positions of all the text and graphic elements that will appear on each page. Of course, the design may be changed as you are working on your project in the desktop publishing program.

There are countless ways to design a document. Professional designing requires education and skill, but you do not have to be a professional designer to create simple, attractive

publications in your desktop publishing software. The exercises in this book will give you the general guidelines you need for document design, as well as ideas to consider and examples to follow. Looking at different publications will give you other ideas to try.

Desktop publishing software often comes with sample documents, or *templates*, already designed and formatted for you. Your software may provide templates for letters, memos, newsletters, reports, and other common documents. Templates can be used as is or modified as needed. You will learn more about templates later in this text.

When you begin to design a publication, try different typefaces, type styles, type sizes, and leading options. Change the margins, and vary the space between columns. Stretch your text boxes to varying lengths. Don't be afraid to experiment! If you are not happy with your work, delete the story, or close your desktop publishing file without saving it and place the file again. You can place files as many times as you like without altering them.

LESSON 4: WORKING WITH IMPORTED TEXT

EXERCISE 31

DISK FILES: SEATRIP (template file)

LEVEL: 2+

LEARNING OBJECTIVES:

> Work with multi-page documents
> Reset tabs
> Use the paragraph feature to adjust spacing

TEACHING SUGGESTIONS:

- Demonstrate how to set tabs in desktop publishing software. Emphasize that students may want to adjust tabs set in the word processor when working with different typefaces and type sizes.

- Demonstrate the paragraph feature in desktop publishing software for creating left indents and right indents and for adding space above and below paragraphs. Emphasize that the space is added to the leading. The space above and below feature, rather than double spacing, is used by professional desktop publishers to add space between paragraphs. The hanging indent feature will be discussed in Exercise 34.

- Demonstrate how to adjust text columns so that the bottom of the text is even, as in the exercise on page 51 of the student text.

- For the exercise, you may need to remind students of how to drag-place text.

SETTINGS:

> .75" margins

SOLUTION:

> As shown in the student text. Note that the solution has been reduced because of space constraints. Line endings may be different. Students should have adjusted text for hyphenation rules. Page 1 should have a 1-point border extending around the text outside the margins. The page should have 3 columns with a .25" gutter. An 8-point line should appear 2.5" from the top of the page and extend across the border. The first-page heading should be in a sans serif typeface with auto leading, right-aligned, 12-point for the first two lines and 30-point for the last two. Hairline rules should appear in the center of the gutters and extend from the 8-point line to the bottom of the border. Body text should be in a serif typeface, 12/18, with a .25" tab. The leading may be less. Students should have aligned the columns at the bottom of page 1. On page 2, students should have set custom columns, with a .25" gutter and the second column beginning 2.5" from the edge of the page. The address information should be in a serif typeface, 9/13, center-aligned, with .01" left indent and .008" right indent. It should appear in a 10% shaded box with a 2-point line. The tour information should be in the same font as the rest of the body text, although students may have adjusted leading to fit the information. The headings should be in a sans serif font, 14/18, with .29" space above and .08" space below.

LESSON 4: WORKING WITH IMPORTED TEXT

EXERCISE 32

DISK FILES: SEATRIP (template file)

LEVEL: 2

LEARNING OBJECTIVES:

Work with multi-page documents
Work with a master page

TERMS: master pages, feathering

TEACHING SUGGESTIONS:

- Explain that a **master page** is used for repeating elements. Text, graphics, and guides placed on the master page(s) will appear on every page of the publication.

- Using a multi-page publication, demonstrate the master page feature in your software. Show students how to access a master page and how to set elements on it. Go to several publication pages and show how the master page elements appear. Show students that they cannot alter master page text or graphic elements, but that they can customize master page guides.

- Show students how to deselect master page elements on publication pages. If your software has separate features for deselecting printing and nonprinting items, demonstrate them. Show students how to use a box with paper fill and no border to hide selected master page elements on publication pages.

- Demonstrate how to set up automatic page numbering in your software.

- Demonstrate **feathering** to lengthen a column of text so that the last lines of two columns end even with each other. Feathering can involve adding a small amount of space after selected paragraphs or increasing the leading slightly.

SETTINGS:

1.5" left and right margins; 1" top and bottom margins.

SOLUTION:

As shown in the text. The solution has been reduced because of space constraints. Line endings and column endings may be different. Students should have adjusted text for hyphenation rules. All pages should have a hairline box extending to the top and bottom margins and 1/4" outside the left and right margins, an 8-point horizontal rule placed as shown, and a running foot placed as shown in a sans serif typeface, 8-point, and centered, with five spaces separating the four elements as shown. The heading on page 1 should be centered horizontally and vertically. The first two lines should be 12/12; the last two, 30/30. The text should be in a sans serif typeface; "presents" should have .2" of space after it. Body text should be 12/16 with .097" of space after paragraphs and should be placed as shown. Students may have had to feather paragraphs so text aligns at the bottom. The third page should have a custom column beginning 3" from the left margin. The tour text should be in that column and should be in a sans serif typeface, italic, 11/13, with no space after paragraphs and justified. The headings should be sans serif 12/12 with .1" of space before and .06" of space after.

LESSON 4: WORKING WITH IMPORTED TEXT

EXERCISE 33

DISK FILES: **TEAM1** (data file), **TEAM** (template file)

LEVEL: 2

LEARNING OBJECTIVES:

> Learn block business letter format
> Use reference initials
> Convert quotes and apostrophes
> Key em and en spaces
> Use paragraph rules

TERMS: reference initials, em space, en space, paragraph rule, footer

PREPARATION/MATERIALS:

Before the class session, check in the manual for your desktop publishing software as to whether quotation marks and apostrophes can be converted automatically to true typeset marks when word-processed files are imported. Test the import feature with a template file.

TEACHING SUGGESTIONS:

- Introduce the block business letter. Go through the formatting and letter parts, referring to the model on page 59 of the student text.

- Make sure students understand true typeset apostrophes and quotation marks. Demonstrate how to key them in classroom software. If classroom software has a feature for converting these marks automatically when word-processed files are imported, show students where this feature is located and how to activate it.

- Demonstrate how to key em and en spaces in classroom software.

- If classroom software has a paragraph rule feature, demonstrate its use.

SETTINGS:

Default.

SOLUTION:

As shown on page 59 of the student text. Note that the solution has been reduced because of space constraints. Body text should be 11/13. The body of the letter should begin 2" from the top of the page. All apostrophes and quotation marks should be true typeset marks (two in Paragraph 1, one in Paragraph 2, four in Paragraph 3 with the inserted quote, one in Paragraph 4, and one in Paragraph 5).

EXERCISE 34

DISK FILES: HEARINGS (template file)

LEVEL: 2

LEARNING OBJECTIVES:

Format text with bullets
Use hanging indents

TERMS: bullets, hanging indent

TEACHING SUGGESTIONS:

- Go over the uses of bullets given on page 60 of the student text.

- Demonstrate how to create bullets in classroom software. If software has features for both manual and automatic bullet creation, demonstrate both. If symbol typefaces are available, demonstrate using symbol characters as bullets. Students could also practice creating boxes or circles with graphic tools to use as bullets.

- Show students how to create a hanging indent in classroom software.

SETTINGS:

All margins should be 1".

SOLUTION:

As shown on page 61 of the student text. Note that the solution has been reduced because of space constraints. Body text should be 11/12. The body of the letter should be centered vertically. Bullets should be indented .5" from the left margin of the letter. The text following the bulleted items should be indented .75" from the left margin of the letter. Students can use the bullet character of their choice.

LESSON 5: WORKING WITH GRAPHICS

○ **EXERCISE 35**

DISK FILES: Students will need four clip art files for this exercise.

LEVEL: 1

LEARNING OBJECTIVES:

Import, resize, and move graphics

TERMS: clip art

PREPARATION/MATERIALS:

Students will need four clip art files for this exercise. You may wish to examine the legal restrictions on use for classroom clip art package(s), since the text discusses legal restrictions. You will need to determine from what location you would like students to import clip art files. Placing the files from a subdirectory or folder on the hard drive will make the work go faster.

TEACHING SUGGESTIONS:

○
- Define **clip art** and discuss sources of clip art. Emphasize that students should carefully examine the legal restrictions on use for any clip art package they purchase. Generally, clip art can be used in a publication if the clip art publisher has been credited and is the copyright owner of the images. You cannot make copies of clip art to distribute to others. With some clip art services, you pay for the right to use images or modify them. Discuss any legal restrictions on use of classroom clip art package(s).

- Emphasize the similarities between placing graphics and placing text, and between working with imported graphics and working with drawn graphics. Placing imported graphics is like placing imported text. The commands for moving, copying, pasting, resizing, deleting, grouping, aligning, and distributing imported graphics are generally the same as those for working with drawn graphics.

- Show students how to place, move, copy, paste, and delete imported graphics. Show students both proportional and disproportional sizing. Explain that, unless they are trying to achieve a special effect, proportional sizing is best.

- If your software has options for grouping, aligning, and distributing graphics, demonstrate these options.

- Show students how to navigate to the location where the clip art files for the exercise will be stored.

SETTINGS:

All margins should be 1″.

SOLUTION:

○
As shown on page 63 of the student text. Students should submit one document each for Part 1 and Part 2 of the exercise. Graphics should be placed and sized as shown. Of course, students may use different graphics.

EXERCISE 36

DISK FILES: SEATRIP2 (data file). Students will need four to six clip art files on vacations in tropical climates (see subject matter of **SEATRIP2**) for this exercise.

LEVEL: 1

LEARNING OBJECTIVES:

Know sources of artwork for desktop publishing
Understand graphics formats
Import, resize, and move graphics

TERMS: text art, screen captures, scanning, resolution

PREPARATION/MATERIALS:

Students will need four to six clip art files for this exercise. The clip art files, which will be used to illustrate the previously prepared data file **SEATRIP2,** should be on the subject of vacations in tropical climates. You may wish to provide examples from publications of some of the different types of art discussed in the Concepts (page 64 of the student text). If possible, have one example of art created in a paint program and one example of art created in a draw program for students to compare.

TEACHING SUGGESTIONS:

- Discuss the different types of artwork that can be used in desktop publishing programs. If you have examples from publications of some of the different types of art, show them to the class. Remind students that they have already learned how to draw objects and use clip art. Discuss text art (raised and dropped capital letters, shadow boxes, rotated text, and so on), paint programs, draw programs, PostScript-based illustration programs, and scanning.

- Many computers come with simple paint and draw programs. If you have access to such a program, consider allowing students to spend some time experimenting with it.

- You may wish to demonstrate how to make a screen capture on classroom computers. Many operating systems and operating environments have a simple method for screen captures that works across programs. Captures often go to the clipboard and can be pasted from there into a desktop publishing document. Students can also bring their captures into a paint program and save them in one of several popular graphics file formats.

- Discuss copyright issues for screen captures and scanned images. Screen shots produced from copyrighted software are also copyrighted. They can be used for examples or in-house training manuals. To use a screen shot from copyrighted software in a publication, you must obtain permission from the copyright holder. When an image is scanned for private use and not for general publication, copyright violations may not be an issue. To scan and use a copyrighted image, you must obtain permission from the copyright holder.

- Emphasize that not all desktop publishing software will read all graphic file formats.

SETTINGS:

1.5" left and right margins; 1" top and bottom margins.

SOLUTION:

As shown on page 65 of the text. Graphics should be placed between the two ruler guides as shown. Students may use different graphics, use different numbers of graphics, and place them differently as long as they are within the guides. Students will submit copies of pages 1 and 2 only. For information about aspects of the solution other than the graphics, see Exercise 32.

LESSON 5:   WORKING WITH GRAPHICS

EXERCISE 37

DISK FILES: **PF1** (data file), two clip art files

LEVEL: 1

LEARNING OBJECTIVES:

Use text flow and text wrap options

TERMS: text wrap, text flow, no wrap, column break, jump over, wrap all sides,
offset/boundary/standoff

PREPARATION/MATERIALS:

Students will need two clip art files.

TEACHING SUGGESTIONS:

- Demonstrate the different text wrap and text flow options available in classroom software.
Make sure students can identify the offset; demonstrate how to change it.

SETTINGS:

Default.

SOLUTION:

As shown on page 67 of the student text. Note that the solution has been reduced because of
space constraints. Students should have placed two graphics. Text in the left column should
break to the next column after the graphic. Text in the right column should jump over the
graphic. Students may use different graphics, of course. Students should have made sure that
text does not break awkwardly and should have deleted text at the end of the story so that it
does not extend below the bottom margin. For other details about the document, see Exercise
28.

EXERCISE 38

DISK FILES: PF1 (data file), one clip art file

LEVEL: 1

LEARNING OBJECTIVES:

Use text flow and text wrap options
Perform a custom wrap

PREPARATION/MATERIALS:

Students will need one clip art file.

TEACHING SUGGESTIONS:

■ Demonstrate custom wrap.

SETTINGS:

Default.

SOLUTION:

As shown on page 69 of the student text. Note that the two solutions have been reduced
because of space constraints. Students may use different graphics, of course. Students should
have made sure that text does not break awkwardly. For the exercise on the left, students
should have adjusted the bottom windowshade handle on the right column so text does not
extend below the bottom margin. For the exercise on the right, students should have deleted
text at the end of the story so that it does not extend below the bottom margin. For other details
about the documents, see Exercise 28.

LESSON 5: WORKING WITH GRAPHICS

EXERCISE 39

DISK FILES: **PF1** (data file)

LEVEL: 2

LEARNING OBJECTIVES:

Create a pull quote
Perform custom wraps

TERMS: placeholder, pull quote

PREPARATION/MATERIALS:

You may wish to bring in examples of pull quotes in publications for students to examine.

TEACHING SUGGESTIONS:

- Discuss the use of **placeholders** to reserve a place for graphics that will come later. They are used when planning a document and for documents that will be produced more than once, such as newsletters.

- Discuss the use of **pull quotes** to attract a reader to a story. If you have brought in examples of pull quotes in publications, circulate them.

- If classroom software allows you to wrap text around grouped objects, demonstrate this option.

- If classroom software allows you to wrap text around drawn graphics, demonstrate this option.

SETTINGS:

Default.

SOLUTION:

As shown on page 71 of the student text. Note that the two solutions have been reduced because of space constraints. For both solutions, students should have made sure that text does not break awkwardly and should have deleted text at the end of the story so that it does not extend below the bottom margin. Students may have chosen a different quote from the text. The type size and leading of the pull quote will vary. For other details about the documents, see Exercise 28.

LESSON 5: WORKING WITH GRAPHICS

EXERCISE 40

DISK FILES: **PF1** (data file), one clip art file

LEVEL: 1

LEARNING OBJECTIVES:

Crop and pan graphics
Follow guidelines for cropping

TERMS: cropping, panning

PREPARATION/MATERIALS:

Students will need a clip art file.

TEACHING SUGGESTIONS:

- Demonstrate cropping and panning on classroom software.

- Go over the guidelines for cropping an image on page 72 of the student text.

SETTINGS:

Default.

SOLUTION:

As shown on page 73 of the student text. Note that the solution has been reduced because of space constraints. Students should have made sure that text does not break awkwardly and should have deleted text at the end of the story so that it does not extend below the bottom margin. The graphic may vary, of course. For other details about the document, see Exercise 28.

LESSON 5: WORKING WITH GRAPHICS

● **EXERCISE 41**

DISK FILES: Students will need four clip art files of animals that might be found in a zoo.

LEVEL: 2

LEARNING OBJECTIVES:

Mask graphics

TERMS: mask

PREPARATION/MATERIALS:

Students will need four clip art files of animals that might be found in a zoo.

TEACHING SUGGESTIONS:

■ If classroom software has a masking option, demonstrate its use.

SETTINGS:

Default.

● **SOLUTION:**

As shown on page 75 of the student text. Note that the solution has been reduced because of space constraints. An 8-point line should be used for the border. Squares should be 1" with a 2-point line and should have .25" of space between them. Graphics, of course, will vary. Students have been instructed to write new copy for the four illustrations to match their graphics. They have been told to try cropping the graphics if classroom software does not have a masking option.

LESSON 5: WORKING WITH GRAPHICS

EXERCISE 42

DISK FILES: Students will need four to eight clip art files relating to business.

LEVEL: 2

LEARNING OBJECTIVES:

Rotate objects
Place inline graphics

TERMS: rotate, inline graphic, ellipsis marks

PREPARATION/MATERIALS:

Students will need four to eight clip art files relating to business. You may need to edit the text of the exercise to match the graphics files available and the capabilities of classroom equipment. See page 77 of the student text.

TEACHING SUGGESTIONS:

- If classroom software has a rotate option, demonstrate its use.

- If classroom software allows you to place or paste objects as inline graphics, demonstrate how this is done.

- Allow students considerable time to practice the rotate and inline graphics options.

- Make sure students understand that ellipsis marks represented omitted material and that they may be used at the end of a sentence that is intended to trail off, with no end-stop punctuation.

SETTINGS:

Default.

SOLUTION:

As shown on page 77 of the student text. Note that the solution has been reduced because of space constraints. The first line of the "Instead of" text block should be 3.5" base to base from the top margin of the document, not the top of the page. The first line of the "The Roberts" text block should be 7.5" base to base from the top margin of the document, not the top of the page. Graphics, of course, will vary in type and number. Students have been instructed to edit the text to match the graphics available. Any changes you have made to the exercise (see "Preparation/Materials" above) should of course be reflected in the solution.

LESSON 5:   WORKING WITH GRAPHICS

● **EXERCISE 43**

DISK FILES: Students will need one clip art file relating to sports.

LEVEL: 2

LEARNING OBJECTIVES:

> Skew objects
> Reflect objects
> Use the graphics control palette

TERMS: skew, reflect, negative leading

PREPARATION/MATERIALS:

> Students will need one clip art file relating to sports. You may need to edit the exercise to match the capabilities of classroom equipment. See page 79 of the student text. You may also wish to show "before" and "after" examples of text with negative leading. See the last bulleted item below.

TEACHING SUGGESTIONS:

- If classroom software has a graphics control palette, show students how to display it and identify the different functions it controls.

- If classroom software has a skew option, demonstrate its use.

- If classroom software has a reflect option, demonstrate its use.

- Allow students some time to practice the skew and reflect graphics options.

- Show students how to produce a copyright symbol on classroom software.

- Discuss the concept of **negative leading.** If possible, show students some text in which negative leading should be set; then show them the same text with negative leading.

SETTINGS:

> Default.

SOLUTION:

> As shown on page 79 of the student text. Coupons should measure 6" by 2.5", should have a 2-point line, and can be located anywhere on the page. Students have not been instructed on exact placement of elements. The graphic, of course, will vary. In the second coupon, students have been instructed to edit the "CAPRUS ATBs" text to match the graphic available. Any changes you have made to the exercise (see "Preparation/Materials" above) should of course be reflected in the solution.

EXERCISE 44

DISK FILES: —

LEVEL: 2

LEARNING OBJECTIVES:

Create a table using desktop publishing software

TERMS: table editor, keyline, monospace, proportional

TEACHING SUGGESTIONS:

- Go over the formatting guidelines for tables, as presented on page 80 of the student text.

- If students will produce the table in the exercise using the **keyline** method, demonstrate it.

- Make sure students understand the difference between **monospace** and **proportional** type.

- Tables can be created in any desktop publishing software, regardless of whether it has a table editor feature. The instructions for this exercise are set up for creating a table in desktop publishing software. The instructions for Exercise 45 are set up for creating a table in the table editor. Both this exercise and Exercise 45 can be formatted using either feature; if you prefer to have students produce both tables in a table editor, or if classroom software has no table editor and you will have students produce both tables in their desktop publishing software, they can follow the general guidelines for desktop publishing software (Exercise 44) or table editors (Exercise 45) for both exercises.

SETTINGS:

1" margins

SOLUTION:

As shown on page 81 of the student text. The table should be centered horizontally and vertically on the page. A rectangle with an attractive border should frame the margins.

EXERCISE 45

DISK FILES: —

LEVEL: 2

LEARNING OBJECTIVES:

Create a table using the table editor

PREPARATION/MATERIALS:

You may wish to familiarize yourself with the table editor feature in classroom software. Decide in what format students will save their files, and determine how they should import them into their desktop publishing software.

TEACHING SUGGESTIONS:

- If your software does not have a table editor feature, students can complete this exercise generally following the instructions for Exercise 44. If students will complete this exercise on desktop publishing rather than table editor software, go over the method for centering column headings over columns described on page 82 of the student text.

- If classroom software has a table editor feature, introduce it. Make sure students understand what a row, a cell, and a column are. Go through the table setup options, including how to set the space between columns. Show students how to select rows, columns, cells, and the entire table. Show them how to turn off and modify table borders. Make sure students know how to group cells.

- Explain the importance of Step 7 to students. Tables are created with a set width. The table editor automatically allocates the width of the table among the four columns. If a table is narrower than the setup width, students can end up with more space between columns than they want, and column headings will not center accurately. A good method for getting around this problem is to set the space between columns you want, key the table, and then drag the columns as described in Step 7.

- Tell students what format to use to save their table and how to import it into desktop publishing software.

SETTINGS:

1" margins

SOLUTION:

As shown on page 83 of the student text. The table should be centered horizontally and vertically on the page.

LESSON 5:   WORKING WITH GRAPHICS

EXERCISE 46

DISK FILES: TEAM2 (data file). Students will also need a graphic pertaining to basketball. You may wish to provide another graphic file for students to use in practicing with the image control feature (see the first bulleted item below).

LEVEL: 1

LEARNING OBJECTIVES:

Use the image control feature
Learn modified block business letter format

TERMS: modified block letter

PREPARATION/MATERIALS:

Students will need a graphic pertaining to basketball. You may wish to provide another graphic file for students to use in practicing with the image control feature (see the first bulleted item below).

TEACHING SUGGESTIONS:

- If classroom software has an image control feature, demonstrate its use. Let students import a clip art file and experiment with it, if possible.

- Review the send to back command, if appropriate.

- Introduce the modified block business letter. Go through the formatting and letter parts, referring to the model on page 85 of the student text.

SETTINGS:

Default.

SOLUTION:

As shown on page 85 of the student text. Note that the solution has been reduced because of space constraints. Graphics used, their exact size, and their placement will vary. For details on the solution, see Exercise 33 (page 39 of this manual).

LESSON 5: WORKING WITH GRAPHICS

EXERCISE 47

DISK FILES: **DESSERT** and **OBJECTS** (data files). Students will also need a graphics file relating to desserts.

LEVEL: 1

LEARNING OBJECTIVES:

> Work with multiple open publications
> Copy objects between publications
> Use the image control feature

PREPARATION/MATERIALS:

> Students will need a graphics file relating to desserts.

TEACHING SUGGESTIONS:

- If classroom software allows you to have more than one publication open at a time, demonstrate this option.

- If classroom software allows you to copy objects from one publication to another by dragging, demonstrate this option.

- This is a review exercise. You may wish to go over any of the features in the Learning Objectives that need reinforcement. In addition to the tasks listed in the Learning Objectives, students will set a decimal tab with leaders and will force-justify text.

SETTINGS:

> All margins should be .75".

SOLUTION:

> As shown on page 86 of the student text. Note that the solution has been reduced because of space constraints. The rules are 12-point. The "coffee cup" text should be 38/50 sans serif bold, force-justified. The coffee price text should be 12/auto sans serif bold. The dessert text should be 12/14 sans serif bold, center-aligned. The price "$2.95" at the top of that text should be 15/14 with .125" of space after. Dessert graphics may vary.

EXERCISE 48

DISK FILES: Students will need a graphics file relating to music and a scissors graphics file, if available.

LEVEL: 1

LEARNING OBJECTIVES:

> Perform a custom wrap
> Set indents and tabs
> Rotate a graphic
> Use en spaces

PREPARATION/MATERIALS:

> Students will need a graphics file relating to music; a scissors graphic or symbol (from a symbol typeface), if available; and a check box symbol, if available.

TEACHING SUGGESTIONS:

> ■ This is a review exercise. You may wish to go over any of the features in the Learning Objectives that need reinforcement.

SETTINGS:

> Default.

SOLUTION:

> As shown on page 88 of the student text. Note that the solution has been reduced because of space constraints. Body text should be 12/15, with a left indent of .25" and .185" of space after. Graphics will vary, but text should be wrapped attractively around the graphic, and students should have edited the text if necessary to match the graphic used. The address text should be in 13-point type, with enough space after the telephone number to set the coupon at the bottom of the page as shown. Coupon rules should be half-point. If students do not have a scissors graphic or symbol (48-point), they can omit the scissors. Students will need to set tabs for the check box material. If students do not have a check box symbol, they have been told to draw a box and paste copies as inline graphics or use underlining.

LESSON 5: WORKING WITH GRAPHICS

● **EXERCISE 49**

DISK FILES: Students will need several graphics files to add to a personal library.

LEVEL: 1

LEARNING OBJECTIVES:

> Use the library feature
> Create a personal library

TERMS: library feature

PREPARATION/MATERIALS:

> Students will need several graphics files to add to a personal library.

TEACHING SUGGESTIONS:

- Discuss the usefulness of a library for storing frequently used text and graphic objects.

- If classroom software has a library feature, demonstrate its use. Show students how to create a library, place items in it, organize items, view items, search for items, and retrieve items into a publication.

● **SETTINGS:**

> Default.

SOLUTION:

> Students are instructed to create a library, place half a dozen text and graphic objects in it, and place two of these objects into any desktop-published document. Students then print a copy of the final document. Solutions will vary widely.

LESSON 6: USING SPECIAL EFFECTS AND FEATURES

EXERCISE 50

DISK FILES: PF (template file)

LEVEL: 1

LEARNING OBJECTIVES:

Use spacing techniques to adjust text

TERMS: kerning, tracking, set width

TEACHING SUGGESTIONS:

- Discuss and demonstrate **kerning,** adjusting word and letter space, changing **tracking,** and changing the width of characters through the **set width** function, if available on classroom software.

SETTINGS:

Default.

SOLUTION:

Solutions will vary widely. Students are instructed to start a new document, import the template file **PF,** and experiment with the spacing techniques taught. They then print a copy of their work and close the file without saving.

LESSON 6: USING SPECIAL EFFECTS AND FEATURES

EXERCISE 51

DISK FILES: FUN1 (data file)

LEVEL: 1

LEARNING OBJECTIVES:

> Create drop caps and raised caps
> Insert a page
> Kern text

TERMS: raised cap, drop cap

TEACHING SUGGESTIONS:

> ■ Show students how to create raised and drop caps using classroom software.

> ■ Show students how to insert pages after a publication has been created.

SETTINGS:

> Top and bottom margins .5″, side margins 2″

SOLUTION:

> Solutions appear on the next two pages. For details about the document, see the manual notes for Exercise 27.

EXERCISE 51—SOLUTION (Page 1 of 2):

VACATION MEANS DIFFERENT THINGS TO DIFFERENT PEOPLE

To some, the roar of the ocean waves crashing on the sandy shore means relaxation and enjoyment. To others, a place with grassy, rolling hills enveloping a duck-filled lake in the country is the perfect getaway. There are many different ideas of the ideal vacation.

Those accustomed to a frenetic daily pace may seek a time just to sit back and unwind, rest at home, rent movies, and eat at local restaurants. Others may choose from many different vacation options depending on individual tastes. A getaway to the tropics provides for tanning, resting on the beach, sailing, or snorkeling by day and dancing and dining by night. There is seldom much sight-seeing to do—the purpose of these vacations is to escape to glorious weather and spend a lot of time at the beach. A trip to the country allows one to horseback-ride; golf; drive through fields of multicolored foliage; and take in the pure, clean air. Evenings may be spent sitting around a fireplace or campfire sipping hot cocoa or going to country fairs.

Vacations to big cities usually involve seeing major landmarks and points of interest. Most of the day may be spent touring the metropolis and shopping for souvenirs. Nights may be spent sampling the native cuisine and seeing local night spots.

How people choose to spend their vacation depends on what they find enjoyable. The main goal is always the same: HAVE FUN!

EXERCISE 51—SOLUTION (Page 2 of 2):

VACATION MEANS DIFFERENT THINGS TO DIFFERENT PEOPLE

To some, the roar of the ocean waves crashing on the sandy shore means relaxation and enjoyment. To others, a place with grassy, rolling hills enveloping a duck-filled lake in the country is the perfect getaway. There are many different ideas of the ideal vacation.

Those accustomed to a frenetic daily pace may seek a time just to sit back and unwind, rest at home, rent movies, and eat at local restaurants. Others may choose from many different vacation options depending on individual tastes. A getaway to the tropics provides for tanning, resting on the beach, sailing, or snorkeling by day and dancing and dining by night. There is seldom much sight-seeing to do—the purpose of these vacations is to escape to glorious weather and spend a lot of time at the beach. A trip to the country allows one to horseback-ride; golf; drive through fields of multicolored foliage; and take in the pure, clean air. Evenings may be spent sitting around a fireplace or campfire sipping hot cocoa or going to country fairs.

Vacations to big cities usually involve seeing major landmarks and points of interest. Most of the day may be spent touring the metropolis and shopping for souvenirs. Nights may be spent sampling the native cuisine and seeing local night spots.

How people choose to spend their vacation depends on what they find enjoyable. The main goal is always the same: HAVE FUN!

LESSON 6: USING SPECIAL EFFECTS AND FEATURES

EXERCISE 52

DISK FILES: COUPONS (data file)

LEVEL: 2

LEARNING OBJECTIVES:

Use color to enhance documents

TERMS: colors palette, spot color, color matching system, process color, color separations, registration, registration marks

PREPARATION/MATERIALS:

You may wish to bring to class publications using spot and process color and a color matching system swatch book (perhaps available from the school art department or a commercial printer).

TEACHING SUGGESTIONS:

- If classroom software supports the application of color, demonstrate how colors are applied.

- Define **spot color.** If you have brought publications using spot color, circulate them. Show students how to mix colors. If possible, show them a few colors from a color matching system. If you have brought a color system swatch book to class, circulate it. Perhaps you can show a color from a color matching system swatch book on classroom software and have students compare it to the color in the swatch book. This is a good opportunity to point out that screen colors may not faithfully represent printed colors. Make sure students understand the importance of a color matching system in ensuring that the color they select is the color they will get in the printed document.

- Define **process color.** If you have brought publications using process color, circulate them. Students will not be using process color in this text.

- Make sure students understand the concept of **color separation** and the usefulness of **registration marks.** Draw their attention to the illustration at the bottom of page 93 in the student text. If classroom software has an option to produce registration marks automatically, demonstrate how to select it; if possible, print a color-separated document. If classroom software does not have a registration mark feature, show students how to draw a registration mark and apply the registration color to it. Explain that in multiple-page documents registration marks should be placed on the master page.

SETTINGS:

Default.

SOLUTION:

Students should produce color separations of the coupons shown on page 93 of the student text. If the classroom has a color printer, students should produce a composite version as well. Note that the base color should be blue. For details about the two documents, see the solution comments on Exercise 43 (page 49 of this manual).

EXERCISE 53

DISK FILES: **ZOO** or **PIM** (data files)

LEVEL: 1

LEARNING OBJECTIVES:

Use color to enhance documents

TEACHING SUGGESTIONS:

■ Discuss the design considerations on **page 94** of the student text.

SETTINGS:

Default.

SOLUTION:

Students should produce color separations of either **ZOO** (Exercise 41) or **PIM** (Exercise 42). If the classroom has a color printer, students should produce a composite version as well. Colors and the elements to which they are applied will vary. For details about the two documents, see the solution comments on the two exercises (pages 47 and 48 of this manual).

You may wish to choose some of the better examples to discuss in class.

LESSON 6: USING SPECIAL EFFECTS AND FEATURES

EXERCISE 54

DISK FILES: **PF1** (template file). Students will also need several clip art files.

LEVEL: 1

LEARNING OBJECTIVES:

Use templates

PREPARATION/MATERIALS:

Students will need several clip art files.

TEACHING SUGGESTIONS:

- Introduce the subject of templates. Discuss how templates can save time in producing documents and can help in design.

- If classroom software contains templates, open several. Show students how a copy of the template is opened, rather than the original. Make sure students understand why this is so.

- Point out text and graphics placeholders in classroom templates. Show students how to replace text and graphics placeholders with text and graphics files of their own.

SETTINGS:

Not applicable.

SOLUTION:

Students should print one template with **PF1** replacing a text story and with their own graphics replacing graphics placeholders. Students have been told to delete text at the end of **PF1** if necessary.

LESSON 6: USING SPECIAL EFFECTS AND FEATURES

EXERCISE 55

DISK FILES: **YARDFILL** (data file)

LEVEL: 1

LEARNING OBJECTIVES:

Create a template

TEACHING SUGGESTIONS:

■ Discuss how creating templates can save time in producing documents.

■ Show students how to save a document as a template using classroom software.

SETTINGS:

Default.

SOLUTION:

As shown on page 97 of the student text. Note that the solution has been reduced. For details about the letterhead itself, see the notes for Exercise 24 on page 29 of this manual.

LESSON 7: USING FEATURES FOR LONG DOCUMENTS

EXERCISE 56

DISK FILES: PF (template file)

LEVEL: 1

LEARNING OBJECTIVES:

Use styles to format documents

TERMS: styles feature, style, styles palette, style sheet

TEACHING SUGGESTIONS:

- Introduce the lesson by explaining that, in the next few exercises, students will learn how to use features of their desktop publishing software to format long documents.

- Introduce the styles feature of the classroom desktop publishing program. Define a **style** as a set of formatting instructions that can be applied to a paragraph and, on some software, to selected text. Discuss the usefulness of styles in saving time and effort and promoting consistency.

- Show students how to apply, create, and edit styles.

SETTINGS:

Default.

SOLUTION:

As shown on page 99 of the student text. Note that the solution has been reduced. In the document on the left, body text should be in a serif typeface, 12/18, fully justified, with a tab set at .35". Headings should be in a sans serif typeface, 14/18, bold, flush left, with .25" before and .125" after. In the document on the right, body text should be in a serif typeface, 11/13, flush left, with .185" after and a tab at .3". Headings should be in sans serif 13/13 bold, red, small caps, with .1" of space before and after and a paragraph rule.

LESSON 7: USING FEATURES FOR LONG DOCUMENTS

EXERCISE 57

DISK FILES: HEALTH (template file)

LEVEL: 2

LEARNING OBJECTIVES:

Learn unbound report format
Learn about feasibility reports
Format a long document
Format text with styles
Use top of caps leading
Use the keep with next option

TERMS: unbound reports, textual citation, top of caps leading, keep with option, feasibility report, analysis

PREPARATION/MATERIALS:

To complete the exercise smoothly as written, students will need to have a top of caps leading option. If classroom software does not have that option, you may wish to work through the exercise before the class session and make any changes to the styles to be created that are necessary so that students' solutions will emulate that in the text.

TEACHING SUGGESTIONS:

- Introduce **unbound reports.** Go through the formatting and parts, referring to the description on page 100 of the student text and the model on pages 101 and 103.
- Emphasize that the traditional unbound report format, which uses line spacing (single, double, and quadruple) for different report parts, sometimes does not translate well into desktop publishing, which uses leading measured in points and space after paragraphs. Remind students that they may need to adjust the spacing in their document to emulate that of a traditional unbound report.
- If classroom software has a **top of caps leading** option, show students how to select it.
- Explain that applying the predominant style to all the text, and then applying less-used styles to individual paragraphs, is an efficient method of formatting.
- If classroom software has a **keep with option,** show students how to select it. If it does not, tell students to check in the exercise for side headings isolated at the bottom of the page.
- Discuss feasibility reports and analyses, referring to the information on page 102 of the student text.

SETTINGS:

1" top and bottom margins; default side margins

SOLUTION:

As shown on pages 101 and 103 of the student text. The solution has been reduced. All text should be in a 12-point serif typeface. Body text should be 12/24. Enumerated and references text should be 12/12. Line endings will vary. Students should have adjusted text for violations of hyphenation and, if a keep with text option is not available, for side headings isolated at the bottom of a page. Check carefully to see that the spacing of the different parts of the solution emulates the model.

LESSON 7:   USING FEATURES FOR LONG DOCUMENTS

EXERCISE 58

DISK FILES: HEALTH1 (data file)

LEVEL: 1

LEARNING OBJECTIVES:

Edit a style
Use the table of contents feature
Format a table of contents

TERMS: table of contents, paragraph headings

PREPARATION/MATERIALS:

If classroom software has a feature for generating tables of contents, you may wish to set up a demonstration for students before the class session.

TEACHING SUGGESTIONS:

- Introduce **tables of contents.** Go through the formatting and parts, referring to the description on page 104 of the student text and the model on page 105.

- Emphasize the usefulness of a table of contents feature for long documents. The feature saves time and effort and reduces the chance of inaccuracies.

- If classroom software has a feature for generating tables of contents, demonstrate its use. Show students how to code text for inclusion in the table of contents. Show students how to edit styles; demonstrate choosing the table of contents option. Make sure students understand the pitfalls of basing one style on another: Any changes made to the master style will be carried through automatically to other styles based upon it. Show students how *not* to base one style on another.

- Show students how to generate a table of contents, if that option is available on classroom software. If you can set the title and the format for page number entries in the table of contents dialog box, do so.

- Make sure students understand that tables of contents do not adjust automatically. If they generate a table of contents and subsequently make changes to the document that affect entries or pagination, they will need to generate a new table of contents to reflect these changes.

- Emphasize that students are responsible for reformatting their table of contents text, if necessary, so that it matches the model.

SETTINGS:

1" top and bottom margins; default side margins

SOLUTION:

As shown on page 105 of the student text. The solution has been reduced. All text should be in a 12/24 serif font. The heading should begin at 2" from the top of the page. Check carefully to see that the solution emulates the model.

LESSON 7: USING FEATURES FOR LONG DOCUMENTS

EXERCISE 59

DISK FILES: HEALTH1 (data file)

LEVEL: 2

LEARNING OBJECTIVES:

Compose an index
Use the index feature

TERMS: index

PREPARATION/MATERIALS:

In this exercise, students compose their own index of the **HEALTH1** data file. Resources on indexing might be useful to students. *The Chicago Manual of Style* (The University of Chicago Press) contains an excellent discussion.

If classroom software has a feature for generating indices, you may wish to set up a demonstration for students before the class session.

TEACHING SUGGESTIONS:

- Discuss the usefulness of indices in helping readers locate pertinent topics.

- Go over the guidelines for preparing an index on page 108 of the student text. Make sure students understand that they will be writing their own index. Index writing is a common task of those who produce publications. Writing an index often takes longer than might be anticipated; that is the reason for the assignment to Level 2 of this exercise. Students may want to write their indices outside class and produce them at the next class session.

- If classroom software has an index feature, show students how to code and edit index entries. Some software has a feature for displaying a working index before generation, so students can make changes as they make entries.

- Show students how to generate an index.

- Emphasize the importance of reviewing the index carefully for errors, inconsistencies, and missing material. Unlike a table of contents, an index generally needs a fair amount of work after generation.

SETTINGS:

1" top and bottom margins; default side margins

SOLUTION:

Solutions will vary. Students are composing their own indices, so index contents will vary. Since formatting guidelines for indices vary widely, students have been told to format the index as they like, as long as it is generally consistent with the **HEALTH1** document.

EXERCISE 60

DISK FILES: —

LEVEL: 1

LEARNING OBJECTIVES:

Learn title page format

TERMS: cover or title page

TEACHING SUGGESTIONS:

- Explain that many reports have a **cover** or **title page.** Go over the traditional format described and illustrated on page 108 of the student text.

SETTINGS:

1″ top and bottom margins; default side margins

SOLUTION:

As shown on page 108 of the student text. Note that the solution has been reduced. Text should be 12/24.

LESSON 8: FORMATTING CORRESPONDENCE

EXERCISE 61

DISK FILES: Students will need a clip art file relating to travel.

LEVEL: 1

LEARNING OBJECTIVES:

Create a letterhead

DESKTOP TECHNIQUES APPLIED:

Use different fonts, use different alignments, choose a bullet style, use em spaces, import a graphic

PREPARATION/MATERIALS:

Students will need a clip art file relating to travel. You may also wish to bring in, or have students bring in, examples of different logos.

TEACHING SUGGESTIONS:

■ Define **logo.** If you or students have brought examples of logos to class, circulate them.

■ Review desktop techniques as necessary. Some techniques that may need review are force justification, dragging to create a text insertion area (Step 3 of the exercise), different options for bullets, saving a file as a template, and keying em spaces.

SETTINGS:

.75" margins

SOLUTION:

As shown on page 111 of the student text. Note that the solution has been reduced. The text at the top of the page should begin at the top margin (.75" from the top of the page). All text should be in a serif typeface. "VOYAGES" should be in 14-point, should be force-justified across 3" at the center of the page, and should have .185" of space after. The rest of the text should be 10-point. "Travel Consultants, Inc." should be center-aligned, with no space after. The address text should begin 1.75" from the top margin and should be italic and flush left. The footer information should be center-aligned. The baseline of the footer should be .75" from the bottom of the page. Bullets may be a different symbol, the desktop publishing software bullet, or a drawn, filled square placed as an inline graphic. An em space should appear before and after each bullet. Graphics, of course, will vary, but should appear in the same location as the graphic in the example and should be sized appropriately.

LESSON 8: FORMATTING CORRESPONDENCE

EXERCISE 62

DISK FILES: —

LEVEL: 1

LEARNING OBJECTIVES:

Create a letterhead
Adjust type and spacing for readability and attractiveness

DESKTOP TECHNIQUES APPLIED:

Draw a filled rectangle, use different fonts, use em spaces and en spaces

TEACHING SUGGESTIONS:

- Go over the design pointers.

- Review the importance of type size and spacing in contributing to the readability and attractiveness of text. Emphasize that decisions on type size and spacing are sometimes a judgment call made during production by the desktop publisher.

- Review desktop techniques as necessary.

SETTINGS:

.5" top and bottom margins, .75" side margins

SOLUTION:

As shown on page 113 of the student text. Note that the solution has been reduced. The rectangle at the top of the page should be at the top margin (.5" from the top of the page), should be centered horizontally, and should be 3.5" long. A similar rectangle should appear .5" from the bottom of the page, again centered horizontally and 3.5" long. All text should be in a sans serif typeface and force-justified. "VISIONIMAGE" should be 18-point, with .35" of space after. The rest of the text should be 9-point, although students have been instructed to change the type size if necessary for readability, attractiveness, and fit. In the address, the spacing between the street and city, and between the ZIP Code and telephone number, should separate the text effectively and contribute to the attractive appearance and readability of the text. The spacing in the footer should perform a similar function. The baseline of the footer should be .25" from the bottom rectangle.

LESSON 8: FORMATTING CORRESPONDENCE

EXERCISE 63

DISK FILES: —

LEVEL: 1

LEARNING OBJECTIVES:

Create a letterhead

DESKTOP TECHNIQUES APPLIED:

Draw a filled circle and rule, use different fonts, use different alignments, add space to paragraphs

TEACHING SUGGESTIONS:

- Go over the design pointer.

- Review desktop techniques as necessary. You may wish to review bringing layered objects to the front and sending them to the back.

SETTINGS:

1" top and bottom margins, .75" side margins

SOLUTION:

As shown on page 115 of the student text. Note that the solution has been reduced. Text should begin 1" from the top and .75" from the left edge of the page. The first line should be 18/auto with .35" of space after. The rest of the address text should be 9/auto. The telephone number should have .125" of space after it. The sponsors and patrons text block should be .75" from the right edge of the page and should end slightly above the bottom margin (1"). The text should be 9/13.5, except for "Sponsors" and "Patrons," which should be 10-point. "Sponsors" and "Patrons" should have .125" of space after; "Patrons" should have .25" of space before. The rule should be 1-point, should be to the left of the sponsors and patrons text as shown, and should extend from just above "Sponsors" to the bottom margin.

LESSON 8: FORMATTING CORRESPONDENCE

EXERCISE 64

DISK FILES: Students will need a graphic file suitable to be the logo for the Holiday Mountain Lodge.

LEVEL: 1

LEARNING OBJECTIVES:

Create a letterhead

DESKTOP TECHNIQUES APPLIED:

Draw a box border, import a graphic, use different fonts, add space to paragraphs, add a paragraph rule

PREPARATION/MATERIALS:

Students will need a graphic file suitable to be the logo for the Holiday Mountain Lodge.

TEACHING SUGGESTIONS:

- Go over the design pointer.

- Review desktop techniques as necessary. You may wish to review re-sizing graphics proportionally and adding paragraph rules.

- If you think it is necessary, make sure students understand Step 8 of the exercise. The graphic will be longer than the text block. Step 8 asks students to move the text block straight up or down so that it is centered vertically opposite the graphic.

SETTINGS:

.75" top and bottom margins, 1" side margins

SOLUTION:

As shown on page 117 of the student text. Note that the solution has been reduced. The margins should be framed by a 1-point box border. The graphic (graphics may vary, of course) should appear 1/8" from the top and left margins and should not extend beyond 3" from the left edge of the page. The text should be in a sans serif typeface, bold, and right-aligned. Text should extend from 3" from the left margin to 7 3/8" from the left margin. The first line should be 18-point and should have .1" of space after. The rest of the text should be 11-point. The last line should have .08" of space after and a 1-point paragraph rule .12" below the baseline. If a paragraph rule feature is not available, students should have drawn the rule 1/8" below the telephone number. The text block should be centered vertically opposite the graphic.

LESSON 8: FORMATTING CORRESPONDENCE

EXERCISE 65

DISK FILES: **ECOLOG** (data file), **CHIMERA** (template file)

LEVEL: 1

LEARNING OBJECTIVES:

> Learn guidelines for the content of a job application letter
> Format a personal-business letter

DESKTOP TECHNIQUES APPLIED:

> Save a file as a template, import a text file, change the font of text

TEACHING SUGGESTIONS:

- You may wish to review the guidelines for formatting personal-business letters and the model letter on pages 20-21 of the student text.

- Go over the guidelines for composing a job application letter that appear on page 118 of the student text.

- The desktop techniques used in this exercise are quite basic and probably will not require review.

SETTINGS:

> Default

SOLUTION:

> As shown on page 119 of the student text. Note that the solution has been reduced. The letter should be in a 10/12 serif font and should be centered vertically on the page. For information on the formatting of the letterhead, see the notes on Exercise 13 (page 15 of this manual).

LESSON 8: FORMATTING CORRESPONDENCE

EXERCISE 66

DISK FILES: **CIRCLE** (data file), **HOLIDAY** (template file)

LEVEL: 1

LEARNING OBJECTIVES:

Format a block business letter

DESKTOP TECHNIQUES APPLIED:

Drag-place a text file, change the font of text

TEACHING SUGGESTIONS:

- You may wish to review the guidelines for formatting business letters and the model letter on pages 58-59 of the student text.

- You may wish to review drag-placing text.

SETTINGS:

1" top and bottom; .75" left and right

SOLUTION:

As shown on page 121 of the student text. Note that the solution has been reduced. The letter should be in a 12/14 serif font, should be justified, and should be centered vertically on the page. For information on the formatting of the letterhead, see the notes on Exercise 63 (page 71 of this manual).

LESSON 8: FORMATTING CORRESPONDENCE

EXERCISE 67

DISK FILES: IMAGE (data file), DESIGN (template file)

LEVEL: 2

LEARNING OBJECTIVES:

> Learn about special letter parts
> Format a block business letter

DESKTOP TECHNIQUES APPLIED:

> Change the font of text, choose a bullet style, insert bullets, space text attractively

TEACHING SUGGESTIONS:

- Explain the purpose and formatting of the different special parts that may appear in a letter, referring to pages 122-123 of the student text. Remind students that, ordinarily, all these letter parts would not appear in one letter.

- You may wish to review procedures for creating bullets on classroom software (e.g., symbol typeface or special character in the desktop software). If students will use any of the following features in placing bullets, you may wish to review them: the inline graphic feature, the power paste feature, or the align and distribute feature.

SETTINGS:

> .5" top and bottom margins; 1" side margins

SOLUTION:

> As shown on page 123 of the student text. Note that the solution has been reduced. The letter should be in an 11/13 serif font and should be centered vertically on the page. Bullet characters and the spacing after them will vary. For information on the formatting of the letterhead, see the notes on Exercise 62 (page 70 of this manual).

LESSON 8: FORMATTING CORRESPONDENCE

EXERCISE 68

DISK FILES: **LODGE** (data file), **GETAWAY** (template file). Students will also need four sports graphics.

LEVEL: 1

LEARNING OBJECTIVES:

Format a modified block business letter with special parts

DESKTOP TECHNIQUES APPLIED:

Import text and graphics files, change the font of text

PREPARATION/MATERIALS:

Students will need four sports graphics.

TEACHING SUGGESTIONS:

- You may wish to review the guidelines for formatting modified block business letters and the model letter on pages 84-85 of the student text.

- Go over the formatting of special letter parts (pages 122-123 of the student text) as necessary.

- You may wish to review procedures for resetting tabs. The other desktop techniques employed in this exercise probably will not require review.

SETTINGS:

.75" top and bottom margins; 1" side margins

SOLUTION:

As shown on page 125 of the student text. Note that the solution has been reduced. The letter should be in an 11/13 serif font and should be centered vertically on the page. Tab settings should be at a half-inch and at the midpoint of the page. Graphics, of course, may vary. Students have been instructed to edit the centered list if necessary to match the graphics available.

LESSON 8:   FORMATTING CORRESPONDENCE

EXERCISE 69

DISK FILES: EARTH (template file). If possible, students should have a graphic or a symbol from a symbol typeface suitable for the logo, as shown on page 127.

LEVEL: 2

LEARNING OBJECTIVES:

> Create a letterhead
> Format a modified block business letter with special parts
> Insert a table into a letter

DESKTOP TECHNIQUES APPLIED:

> Format text in different fonts, rotate text, draw rules and boxes, reset tabs, create a table

PREPARATION/MATERIALS:

> If possible, students should have a graphic or a symbol from a symbol typeface suitable for the logo, as shown on page 127.

TEACHING SUGGESTIONS:

> ■ Go over the formatting of second-page headings in letters and of tables in letters (page 126 of the student text).
>
> ■ This is an intensive exercise. You may wish to review procedures for rotating text, for inserting inline graphics, and particularly for creating tables (pages 80-83 of the student text). If students are using a table editor, make sure they know how to import a table created in the table editor into a desktop-published document.

SETTINGS:

> .75" left and top margins; 1" right and bottom margins

SOLUTION:

> As shown on page 127 of the student text. Note that the solution has been reduced. The rotated text should be 39-point. Graphics, of course, will vary; students may not have a graphic. The address text at the upper right should be 12/auto. A bullet created in the desktop publishing software should separate the street and city and the two telephone numbers. En spaces should be set on either side of the bullet. Both rules should be 1-point. The vertical rule should be 1 5/8" in from the left edge of the page and should extend from the top (.75") to the bottom (1") margins. The horizontal rule should be 1.25" down from the top of the page and should extend from the vertical rule to the right margin (1"). The letter should be 12/14 with a .5" tab for the first lines of paragraphs and a tab set at the midpoint of the page for the date and closing lines. Students should have set a tab for the "Enclosures" text equal to about two spaces. The text on page 1 should begin 2" from the top of the page. The heading on page 2 should be 12/14 and should begin 1" from the top of the page. The body text on that page should be adjusted so that it looks as though a double space separates the heading from the text. The table should be centered horizontally. A double space should separate the table from text above and below. The table text is in an 11/22 sans serif font, except for the first two lines, which are 12/22. Column heads should be blocked. The figures in Column 2 should be right-aligned. Students keying the table in their desktop publishing software have been instructed to leave ten spaces between the two columns when creating the keyline.

LESSON 8: FORMATTING CORRESPONDENCE

EXERCISE 70

DISK FILES: **CIRCLE** (data file), **CAMMEMO** (template file). Students will also need a few graphics relating to December holidays or parties.

LEVEL: 1

LEARNING OBJECTIVES:

Learn standard memo format
Create a memo form
Format a memo

DESKTOP TECHNIQUES APPLIED:

Save a file as a template, import text and graphics files, change the font of text

PREPARATION/MATERIALS:

Students will need a few graphics relating to December holidays or parties.

TEACHING SUGGESTIONS:

- Introduce the standard memorandum. Go through the formatting and special parts, referring to the information and model on pages 128-129 of the student text.

- The desktop techniques employed in this exercise probably will not require review.

SETTINGS:

.75" side margins; 1" top and bottom margins

SOLUTION:

As shown on page 129 of the student text. Note that the solution has been reduced. The memo should be in a 12/14 serif font. Graphics, of course, may vary.

LESSON 8: FORMATTING CORRESPONDENCE

EXERCISE 71

DISK FILES: **VOYAGES** (data file), **AIR** (template file)

LEVEL: 1

LEARNING OBJECTIVES:

Create a memo form
Format a memo

DESKTOP TECHNIQUES APPLIED:

Save a file as a template, import a text file, change the font of text, create a table

TEACHING SUGGESTIONS:

■ You may wish to review procedures for creating tables (pages 80-83 of the student text). In this exercise, the table column heads are longer than the column text. Students creating their tables in desktop publishing software have been told to key the column headings center-aligned with 16 spaces between them (they do not need to set tabs for the column headings). In both desktop publishing software and a table editor, students will need to set a tab for each column, check visually as to whether the tab centers the longest line in the column under the column heading, and adjust the tab as needed. If students are using a table editor, make sure they know how to import a table created in the table editor into a desktop-published document.

SETTINGS:

All margins should be .75" except the bottom margin, which should be 1".

SOLUTION:

As shown on page 131 of the student text. Note that the solution has been reduced. The memo should be in a 12/14 serif font, except for the table, which should be 12/12. The memo text should begin 2" from the top of the page. Students keying the table in their desktop publishing software have been instructed to leave 16 spaces between the two columns.

LESSON 8: FORMATTING CORRESPONDENCE

EXERCISE 72

DISK FILES: FAX (template file)

LEVEL: 1

LEARNING OBJECTIVES:

Learn simplified memo format
Format a memo

DESKTOP TECHNIQUES APPLIED:

Import a text file, change the font of text

TEACHING SUGGESTIONS:

- Introduce the simplified memorandum. Go through the formatting, referring to the information and model on pages 132-133 of the student text.

- The desktop techniques employed in this exercise probably will not require review.

SETTINGS:

All margins should be at the default settings except for the bottom margin, which should be 1".

SOLUTION:

As shown on page 133 of the student text. Note that the solution has been reduced. "INTEROFFICE MEMORANDUM" should be in a 14-point bold sans serif font and should appear 1" from the top of the page. The memo should be in an 11/13 serif font and should begin 2" from the top of the page.

LESSON 8: FORMATTING CORRESPONDENCE

EXERCISE 73

DISK FILES: HOUSE (template file)

LEVEL: 2

LEARNING OBJECTIVES:

Format a memo

DESKTOP TECHNIQUES APPLIED:

Draw filled rectangles, add bullets and en spaces, add space to paragraphs, drag-place text, set text in columns, adjust text blocks

TEACHING SUGGESTIONS:

- You may wish to review the following desktop techniques: setting up columns, adjusting bottom windowshade handles, drag-placing text, moving text blocks, and keying bullets and en spaces in desktop publishing software. If students have a multiple paste feature with horizontal offset, or an align and distribute option, you may want to review that option, since they could use it to paste the copy of the rectangle (Step 19). The example uses a horizontal offset of 3.625″.

SETTINGS:

All margins should be .1″ except for the top margin, which should be 75″.

SOLUTION:

As shown on page 135 of the student text. Note that the solution has been reduced. The text at the top should be 30-point bold with a left indent of .125″. Body text should be 12/auto and should begin at just under 2″ on the vertical ruler. The house description text should be set in two columns with a .75″ gutter. All house description text should have a .125″ left indent. City and state text should be 14/auto bold. The rest of the house description text should be 10/auto. Students should have added .05″ before "CHAPPAQUA" and after each house price, "Greenhouse," and "5 1/2 baths." Students should have added .135″ after the two states. A desktop publishing software bullet and en space should appear before each house description detail, as shown. Approximately a double space should separate the house descriptions from the last paragraph of body text.

LESSON 9: FORMATTING REPORTS

EXERCISE 74

DISK FILES: HEALTH (template file)

LEVEL: 2+

LEARNING OBJECTIVES:

Create a bar or pie chart, format a report

DESKTOP TECHNIQUES APPLIED:

Use a master page, create styles, kern text, draw rules and filled boxes, cut and paste text and objects, drag-place text

TEACHING SUGGESTIONS:

- Introduce the hanging indent style for enumerated items and the endnotes method of referencing sources, referring to the information on page 136 of the text. Make sure students understand that they must produce both an endnotes page and a separate references page.
- Discuss elements and different types of charts, referring to the information on page 138 of the text. Walk students through the creation of a simple chart on available classroom software.
- You may wish to review the following desktop techniques: setting up custom columns, setting up automatic page numbering, defining and applying styles, setting a hanging indent, drag-placing text, hiding master page items (all items and just one on a page), keying superscript numbers, and using the text wrap jump over option.

SETTINGS:

All margins should be .75".

SOLUTION:

As shown on pages 137 and 139 of the student text. The solution has been reduced. A 2-point rule should extend across the top margin on each page except the title page. The title should be in 24-point bold sans serif and should begin 1" from the top of the page. The first paragraph should begin 1.75" from the top of the page. Body text paragraphs should be 11/14 serif, should be indented 3" from the left edge of the page, and should have .125" of space after. The first line of each paragraph should have an additional indent of .35". The first paragraph of each section should begin with a 22/14 bold raised cap. For enumerated text, the number should be in bold; the text following the number should be blocked at 3.594" from the left edge of the page. Side headings should be 12/14 bold sans serif and should appear at the left margin, aligned baseline to baseline with the first lines of the appropriate text sections. Sections should be separated by two line returns, with extra returns when appropriate. Page numbers should be in 10-point bold sans serif and should appear on all pages except the title page and page 1. Students may create either a bar or a pie chart. Charts will vary but should clearly present the information as shown. References and endnotes should appear on separate pages as shown. The heads should be 18/auto bold sans serif caps and should be aligned baseline to baseline with the first line of text. On each page, the baseline of the first line of text should be 1 3/8" from the top of the page. Endnotes should have a first-line indent of .35" and should be in numerical order as shown. References should have a hanging indent of .35". On the title page, the title should be in a 30-point bold sans serif font and should be 2" from the top of the page. The line under the title should be 4-point and should be 2 5/8" from the top of the page. The author/date text should be in a 15/auto bold sans serif font, double-spaced, 8 1/8" from the top of the page, and aligned at the right margin. The rule above the author/date text should be 2-point, should extend from the beginning of the text to the right margin, and should appear 8" from the top of the page. Text should have been checked for violations of hyphenation rules.

LESSON 9: FORMATTING REPORTS

EXERCISE 75

DISK FILES: CASA (template file)

LEVEL: 3

LEARNING OBJECTIVES:

Create a bar or pie chart, format paragraph styles, format a report

DESKTOP TECHNIQUES APPLIED:

Use a master page, create styles, draw rules, ovals, and boxes, generate a table of contents, generate an index

TEACHING SUGGESTIONS:

- Introduce paragraph headings, referring to the information on page 140 of the student text.
- You may wish to review the following desktop techniques: defining and applying styles, setting hanging indents, setting bullets and tabs, using multiple paste/offset or align and distribute features, creating tables and charts, and using index and table of contents features.

SETTINGS:

All margins should be 1".

SOLUTION:

As shown on pages 141, 143, and 145 of the student text. The solution has been reduced. The 1-point box should appear .5" from each edge. The running head should be 10-point sans serif, with an em space between "Report" and the page number. The header should be in italic except for the page number; the page number and "CASA" are bold. The running head sits at the top and right margins; the .5-point rule beneath it should run on the top margin, from the left to the right margin. The running head appears on all pages except the contents and title pages. On the first page, table of contents, references page, and index, text should begin 1.5" from the top of the page. For the report body, the baseline of the first line of text is 1.5" from the top of the page. The title should be sans serif bold, 20/auto for the first line and 18/auto for the second. Side headings should be 14/auto bold/italic sans serif, with a .35" left indent and .125" before and after. Body text should be 12/15 serif and indented 2" from the left edge of the page. In the chart on page 1, ovals should be 1-point, 1.5" by .75", and .25" apart. Their contents should be 9/auto sans serif and aligned in rows baseline to baseline. The center text should be 14/auto bold serif; the lines radiating from it should be 1-point. The table text should be 11/22 sans serif; the title should be 12/22 bold. The top line should be 2-point, the bottom line should be 1-point, and the fill should be 20%. The table should be centered horizontally. Pull quotes should be 18/22 serif italic, with a .35" left indent. The line above should be 2-point; the line below should be 1-point. For bulleted text, the symbol and indent may vary. Charts may be either bar or pie; they may vary but should include the information shown. Paragraph headings should be 12/15 sans serif bold/italic. Funding and board of director information should be serif 11/13 with a .25" left indent, in 2 columns with a .167" gutter. Titles should be bold. Shade and rules should be the same as for the table. References, contents, and index heads should be formatted as side headings. References should have a hanging indent of .5". Index entries should have the default software format. Index contents will vary. Contents entries should have 24-point leading and leaders; page numbers should be right-aligned 1" from the right edge of the page. Contents should include only the listings shown. The title should begin 2.5" from the top of the title page and 1.25" from the left edge. It should have the same formatting as the title on page 1. The 1-point rule below should begin 1" in from each side margin. Text should have no widows or orphans.

LESSON 10: FORMATTING FORMS

EXERCISE 76

DISK FILES: Students will need a graphic or symbol from a symbol typeface for the logo.

LEVEL: 1

LEARNING OBJECTIVES:

Format a form
Learn purchase order format

DESKTOP TECHNIQUES APPLIED:

Key text in different fonts, draw rules, use bullets and en spaces, use symbols or graphics

PREPARATION/MATERIALS:

You may wish to bring in, or have students bring in, examples of different forms that may be created on the desktop for students to examine. Desktop publishing software often has templates for common forms. Students will need a graphic or symbol from a symbol typeface for the logo.

TEACHING SUGGESTIONS:

- Discuss guidelines for formatting forms and purchase orders, referring to the information on page 146 and the model document on page 147 of the student text. If you or students have brought sample forms into class, circulate and discuss them.

- Review the creation of desktop publishing software bullets and en spaces, if necessary.

SETTINGS:

Default

SOLUTION:

As shown on page 147 of the student text. Note that the solution has been reduced. "Tabitha" should be serif 24/auto italic, center-aligned, and should appear at the top margin. The next line should be 12/auto small caps. The first two words of that line should be bold; the rest should be right-aligned. Bullets, with en spaces on either side of them, should appear as shown. All lines should be .5-point except the double rule. The rectangle should appear approximately .5" below the double rule and at the left margin; it should measure 3" by 1". The four lines beginning "PO No." should be sans serif 12/auto bold, right-aligned. The top of that text block should be flush with the top border of the rectangle. "Shipped" should appear about .75" to the right of the right border of the rectangle. "Purchase Order" should be sans serif 12-point bold. Its baseline should be approximately 3/8" from the bottom line of the double rule. It should begin approximately .25" to the right of the colons below. The columned grid should extend from margin to margin and should be 5" deep. Column headings should be centered across each column, should be aligned base to base, and should be sans serif 12/auto bold. The three narrower columns should be 1.25" wide. A rule should appear at the center (3/8" in) of the last two columns as shown. "By" should be sans serif 12/auto bold. Its baseline should align with the rule next to it, which should be 4" long and extend to the right margin.

LESSON 10: FORMATTING FORMS

EXERCISE 77

DISK FILES: PO (data file)

LEVEL: 1

LEARNING OBJECTIVES:

Format a form
Learn invoice format

DESKTOP TECHNIQUES APPLIED:

Key text to replace existing text, use copy and paste features, adjust text blocks and rules, draw a rectangle with fill

TEACHING SUGGESTIONS:

- Discuss guidelines for formatting invoices, referring to the information on page 148 and the model document on page 149 of the student text.

- The desktop techniques used in this exercise probably will not require review.

SETTINGS:

Default

SOLUTION:

As shown on page 149 of the student text. Note that the solution has been reduced. Check that students have correctly keyed the replacement text "Invoice," "Date," "Customer," and "Order No.", as well as the replacement text in the first row. In the first row, check that the first two column heads are correctly center-aligned. The first row should have 60% fill with no line. The "Terms" column should be 1.5" wide. The columnar material should appear .5" below the rectangle. For other details about the creation of the form, see page 84 of this manual.

LESSON 10: FORMATTING FORMS

EXERCISE 78

DISK FILES: Students will need a symbol from a symbol typeface suitable for a check box.

LEVEL: 1

LEARNING OBJECTIVES:

Format a form
Learn survey format

DESKTOP TECHNIQUES APPLIED:

Key text in different fonts, draw rules, set tabs, use em spaces, use symbols or drawn objects

PREPARATION/MATERIALS:

You may wish to bring in, or have students bring in, examples of different surveys that may be created on the desktop. Students will need a symbol from a symbol typeface suitable for a check box.

TEACHING SUGGESTIONS:

- Discuss guidelines for formatting surveys, referring to the information on page 150 and the model document on page 151 of the student text. If you or students have brought sample surveys to class, examine and circulate them.

- Review the following desktop publishing techniques as appropriate and necessary: keying em spaces, setting tabs, using a paragraph rule, using a power paste feature with vertical offset, and obtaining and using a symbol from a symbol typeface.

SETTINGS:

Default

SOLUTION:

As shown on page 151 of the student text. Note that the solution has been reduced. "Todd's" should appear just inside the top and left margins and should be sans serif 36/auto bold. "ELECTRONICS" should be sans serif 14/auto bold. An em space should separate the two words. The two rules should be 4-point. The survey should begin .25" below the bottom rule. The title should be sans serif 14/auto bold, center-aligned. The text should be sans serif 12/ auto. Numbers should be indented .25"; text after numbers should be indented .5"; and the second check box in a row should be indented 3". An em space should separate each check box from the text that follows. All rules should be .5-point. The rules in Question 7 should be .25" apart. The text at the bottom should be sans serif 11/auto, center-aligned, with an em space between the ZIP Code and the telephone number.

LESSON 10: FORMATTING FORMS

EXERCISE 79

DISK FILES: Students will need a symbol from a symbol typeface suitable for a logo and another symbol suitable for a check box.

LEVEL: 1

LEARNING OBJECTIVES:

Format a form

DESKTOP TECHNIQUES APPLIED:

Change the spacing of text, key text in different fonts, use paragraph rules or power paste, use em spaces and en spaces, use symbols or drawn objects

PREPARATION/MATERIALS:

Students will need a symbol from a symbol typeface suitable for a logo and another symbol suitable for a check box.

TEACHING SUGGESTIONS:

- Review the following desktop publishing techniques as appropriate and necessary: using a symbol from a symbol typeface, changing the spacing of text, using paragraph rules, using a power paste feature with vertical offset, and keying em spaces and en spaces.

SETTINGS:

Default

SOLUTION:

As shown on page 153 of the student text. Note that the solution has been reduced. The company title should appear on two lines at the top and right margins and should be 30/30 bold with 120% spacing. Students should have used an appropriate symbol for the logo. The questionnaire should begin approximately 3/8" below the rule. The title of the questionnaire should be sans serif 16/auto bold. Students should double-space here and in the other locations indicated in the solution. The body text should be sans serif 12/24. Subtitles should be 13/24 bold. All rules should be .5-point. For the first seven lines, rules should begin .25" to the right of "Number" and should extend to the right margin. Students should have used an appropriate symbol or drawn object for the check boxes. An en space should follow each check box; an em space should precede each check box except the first. The rules following the numbers should appear .25" in from the left margin and should extend from margin to margin. A quadruple-space should separate the numbered items from the text at the bottom, which should be 12/auto.

LESSON 11: FORMATTING AGENDAS

EXERCISE 80

DISK FILES: AGENDA (template file)

LEVEL: 1

LEARNING OBJECTIVES:

Learn agenda format
Format an agenda

DESKTOP TECHNIQUES APPLIED:

Draw rectangles and rules, import a text file, format text in different fonts, reset a tab

TEACHING SUGGESTIONS:

- Define an **agenda.** Go through the traditional agenda format illustrated on page 154 of the student text.

- The desktop techniques used in this exercise probably will not require review.

SETTINGS:

All margins should be .5" except for the top margin, which should be 1".

SOLUTION:

As shown on page 155 of the student text. Note that the solution has been reduced. "TOTTENVILLE HIGH SCHOOL" should be set in 34-point with .75" after. "PROGRAM" should be in 18-point. The remainder of the heading text as well as "LUNCHEON TO FOLLOW" should be in 14-point. The lines under "PROGRAM" and "Model Office Classroom" should be 8-point. Body text should be in 10-point with a .5" indent from the left margin and a tab at 3.75". The outer framing box should use a 4-point line. It should extend from the left to the right margin (.5" on each side) and from 2" from the top of the page to the bottom margin (.5"). The inner framing box should use an 8-point line. It should extend from .75" in from the left margin to .75" in from the right margin and from 2.25" from the top margin to .75" from the bottom margin.

LESSON 11: FORMATTING AGENDAS

EXERCISE 81

DISK FILES: MEET (template file)

LEVEL: 1

LEARNING OBJECTIVES:

Format an agenda

DESKTOP TECHNIQUES APPLIED:

Create custom columns, format text in different fonts, set a hanging indent, set tracking and character width, create a style based on text

TEACHING SUGGESTIONS:

- Go over the design tips.

- Review the following desktop techniques as necessary: creating custom columns, setting a hanging indent, creating styles, creating styles based on text, changing the tracking of text, changing the character width of text, and formatting text with a paragraph rule.

SETTINGS:

All margins should be .5".

SOLUTION:

As shown on page 157 of the student text. Note that the solution has been reduced. The document should contain two columns, the first ending at 2.5" from the left edge of the page. The gutter should be .167". The text in the left column should be in 24-point with very tight tracking and 70% character width (if available). It should be 4" down from the top of the page and should end 1/8" short of the right edge of the column. The text in the right column should be 1" down from the top of the page. The session numbers should be 24-point with very tight tracking and 70% character width (if available). They should be separated from the following text by an em space. The time text should be 12-point. The rest of the text should be 10-point. The topics should have a .5-point rule extending across the column.

LESSON 12: FORMATTING NEWS RELEASES

EXERCISE 82

DISK FILES: **IMAGE** (data file), **NEWS1** (template file)

LEVEL: 1

LEARNING OBJECTIVES:

Learn news release format
Format a news release

DESKTOP TECHNIQUES APPLIED:

Import a text file, right-align text, change the font of text, set a first indent

PREPARATION/MATERIALS:

You may wish to bring in examples of news releases for students to examine.

TEACHING SUGGESTIONS:

- Discuss the content, organization, and formatting of news releases, referring to the information on page 158 and the model document on page 159 of the student text. If you have brought sample news releases into class, circulate them.

- The desktop techniques used in this exercise probably will not require review.

SETTINGS:

The top and bottom margins should be .5"; the left and right margins should be 1".

SOLUTION:

As shown on page 159 of the student text. Note that the solution has been reduced. The text of the news release should begin 2" from the top of the page. The "For Release" and contact information should be flush right, as shown. Text should be serif 12-point. The first two lines, and the three blank lines after them, should have 12-point leading. The rest of the release should have 24-point leading. The body of the release should have a .5" first-line indent. For information about the letterhead, see the comments on Exercise 62 (page 70 of this manual).

LESSON 12: FORMATTING NEWS RELEASES

EXERCISE 83

DISK FILES: **CIRCLE** (data file), **NEWS2** (template file)

LEVEL: 1

LEARNING OBJECTIVES:

Format a news release

DESKTOP TECHNIQUES APPLIED:

Change the margins of a file, import a text file, change the font of text, set a first indent

TEACHING SUGGESTIONS:

■ The desktop techniques used in this exercise probably will not require review.

SETTINGS:

All margins should be 1".

SOLUTION:

As shown on page 161 of the student text. Note that the solution has been reduced. The text of the news release should begin 2.75" from the top of the page. The "For Release" and contact information should be flush right, as shown. Text should be serif 11-point. The first two lines, and the three blank lines after them, should have 11-point leading. The rest of the release should have 22-point leading. The body of the release should have a .5" first-line indent. For information about the letterhead, see the comments on Exercise 63 (page 71 of this manual).

LESSON 13: FORMATTING RESUMES

EXERCISE 84

DISK FILES: RESUME2 (template file)

LEVEL: 1

LEARNING OBJECTIVES:

Format a resume

DESKTOP TECHNIQUES APPLIED:

Reset tabs, set tracking and character width, insert bullets in text, create and apply a style, add paragraph rules

TEACHING SUGGESTIONS:

- Review the following desktop techniques as appropriate and necessary: resetting tabs, changing the tracking and character width of text, setting paragraph rules, creating a style based on text, and inserting desktop publishing software bullets.

SETTINGS:

The left margin should be 1". All other margins should be .75".

SOLUTION:

As shown on page 163 of the student text. Note that the solution has been reduced. The resume should be placed at the top and left margins. All the text should be sans serif 12/12, except "THOMAS BERGMAN," which should be 14/12 with very loose tracking and 120% character width. "THOMAS BERGMAN" and all the text flush under it should be at 3" from the left edge of the page. Text following bullets, which should be desktop publishing software bullets, should be 3.5" from the left edge of the page. All rules should be 1-point. The side rules should extend to slightly short of the text that begins at 3".

LESSON 13: FORMATTING RESUMES

EXERCISE 85

DISK FILES: RESUME3 (template file)

LEVEL: 1

LEARNING OBJECTIVES:

Learn functional resume format
Format a resume

DESKTOP TECHNIQUES APPLIED:

Import a text file, change the font of text, set left and right indents, create and apply a style, draw rules and boxes

TEACHING SUGGESTIONS:

- Discuss the purpose and contents of functional resumes, referring to pages 164-165 of the student text.

- Review the following desktop techniques as appropriate and necessary: setting left and right indents and creating a style.

SETTINGS:

The left and right margins should be .75". The top and bottom margins should be .5".

SOLUTION:

As shown on page 165 of the student text. Note that the solution has been reduced. The double-line border should frame the margins. All text should be 10-point with a .5" right indent. The name and address information at the top and the headings should be sans serif and indented .5" from the left margin; the rest of the text should be serif and indented 1" from the left margin.

LESSON 13: FORMATTING RESUMES

EXERCISE 86

DISK FILES: **RESUME4** (template file)

LEVEL: 1

LEARNING OBJECTIVES:

Format a resume

DESKTOP TECHNIQUES APPLIED:

Set custom columns, import a text file, reset a tab, cut and paste text, align text baseline to baseline

TEACHING SUGGESTIONS:

- Review the following desktop techniques as appropriate and necessary: setting custom columns, drag-pasting text, setting paragraph rules, resetting tabs, and aligning text baseline to baseline.

SETTINGS:

All margins should be .75".

SOLUTION:

As shown on page 167 of the student text. Note that the solution has been reduced. The lines in the name and address text should be 4-point. The name should be sans serif 13-point, with the first initial of the first, middle, and last names bold. The rest of the address text should be sans serif 11/18. The rest of the text in the resume should be serif 12-point. Headings should be aligned with the appropriate text baseline to baseline as shown. The second column should begin at approximately 2 7/16" from the left edge of the page. The second reference should be indented 2.5" from the beginning of the column.

LESSON 13: FORMATTING RESUMES

EXERCISE 87

DISK FILES: **RESUME5** (template file)

LEVEL: 1

LEARNING OBJECTIVES:

Format a resume

DESKTOP TECHNIQUES APPLIED:

Import a text file, change the font and width of text, create styles based on text, format text with a paragraph rule, draw a filled box

TEACHING SUGGESTIONS:

- Review the following desktop techniques as appropriate and necessary: changing the width of text, setting em spaces, force-justifying text, creating styles based on text, and setting a left indent.

SETTINGS:

The left and right margins should be 2″. The top and bottom margins should be .75″.

SOLUTION:

As shown on page 169 of the student text. Note that the solution has been reduced. The rectangle should be just inside the top, left, and right margins and should be .25″ tall. All text should be sans serif and should have 120% width. The name should be 15/14, with em spaces between the words and force-justified. The address information should be 11/14. The rest of the text should be 10/12. The rules beneath the headings should be hairline and should extend from margin to margin.

LESSON 14: FORMATTING INVITATIONS AND ANNOUNCEMENTS

EXERCISE 88

DISK FILES: Students will need a graphic file relating to food.

LEVEL: 1

LEARNING OBJECTIVES:

Format an invitation

DESKTOP TECHNIQUES APPLIED:

Draw shapes with fills, draw lines, key text in different fonts, import a graphic file, use ruler guides to align text

PRE PARATION/MATERIALS:

Students will need a graphic file relating to food.

TEACHING SUGGESTIONS:

■ Go over the design pointer/hint.

■ Review changing to landscape orientation, if necessary.

SETTINGS:

The page should be landscape orientation. The left and right margins should be 3.5"; the top and bottom margins should be .75".

SOLUTION:

As shown on page 171 of the student text. The rectangle should have a 1-point line and 20% shade. It should frame the margins. The oval should have a 1-point line. It should extend .25" in on each side and should be .25" from the top and bottom of the page. The two lines are 4-point, should be placed to the back as shown, and should be 1" in from the left and right edges of the page and 2" and 4.5" down from the top of the page. The restaurant text should be 12/20 serif small caps and should begin just under 2.5" from the top of the page and 1" from the side of the page. The two sets of restaurant text should be aligned horizontally. The invitation text should be in serif small caps 14/25. Graphics, of course, will vary.

LESSON 14: FORMATTING INVITATIONS AND ANNOUNCEMENTS

EXERCISE 89

DISK FILES: PAUL (data file)

LEVEL: 1

LEARNING OBJECTIVES:

Format an invitation

DESKTOP TECHNIQUES APPLIED:

Use a custom page size, key text in different fonts, copy objects between files, re-size drawn objects, use copy and paste features

TEACHING SUGGESTIONS:

■ Review the following desktop techniques as appropriate and necessary: setting a custom page size, setting left and right indents, force-justifying text, and using a multiple paste feature with offset.

SETTINGS:

The page should be 5″ by 7″. All margins should be .25″.

SOLUTION:

As shown on page 173 of the student text. Text should begin just below the .25″ top margin. "PARTY" should be sans serif 36-point bold, force-justified, with .25″ after. The rest of the text should be 14/14.5 serif. "SIXTEENTH BIRTHDAY" should have .5″ left and right indents, should be bold, and should be force-justified. The rest of the text should be center-aligned. Students should have double-spaced as shown.

Students should have opened the data file **PAUL** and copied a candle from that file. Candles should be 20% gray with no line and should be .25″ wide. All candles should sit on the bottom margin (.25″). Candles should be sized as shown. The first candle is at the left margin (.25″); the fifth is at the right margin (.25″). The distance between candles, in order, is .5″, 1″, 1.25″, and .5″.

LESSON 14: FORMATTING INVITATIONS AND ANNOUNCEMENTS

EXERCISE 90

DISK FILES: Students will need a graphic relating to travel.

LEVEL: 1

LEARNING OBJECTIVES:

Format an invitation

DESKTOP TECHNIQUES APPLIED:

Use a custom page size, use landscape orientation, set tracking and character width, create raised caps, force-justify text

PREPARATION/MATERIALS:

Students will need a graphic relating to travel.

TEACHING SUGGESTIONS:

- Review the following desktop techniques as appropriate and necessary: setting a custom page size, changing to landscape orientation, changing the tracking of text, changing the character width of text, and force-justifying text.

SETTINGS:

The page should be 7" by 6". All margins should be .25".

SOLUTION:

As shown on page 175 of the student text. Students should have drawn a double-line box around the margins (.25"). "Voyages" should be in 72/74, with very loose tracking and a character width of 130%, if available. The line below is 1-point. An appropriate graphic should appear as shown. "Travel Consultants, Inc." should be in a 14/21 serif font, with en spaces rather than spaces between the words. Initial capitals should be 18-point bold. "Travel Consultants, Inc." should be force-justified. The invitation text should be in a 9/22 script or serif italic font.

LESSON 14: FORMATTING INVITATIONS AND ANNOUNCEMENTS

EXERCISE 91

DISK FILES: —

LEVEL: 1

LEARNING OBJECTIVES:

Format an announcement

DESKTOP TECHNIQUES APPLIED:

Use a custom page size, key text in different fonts, force-justify text, draw a filled rectangle and square, copy and paste objects

PREPARATION/MATERIALS:

You may wish to bring in, or have students bring in, examples of announcements.

TEACHING SUGGESTIONS:

- Discuss the purpose and general formatting guidelines for announcements, referring to the information in the Concepts on page 182 of the student text. If you or students have brought in examples of announcements, circulate them.

- Review the following desktop techniques as appropriate and necessary: setting a custom page size, force-justifying text, pasting multiple copies with the offset feature, and aligning and distributing objects.

SETTINGS:

The page should be 5″ by 7″. The left margin should be 2″; all other margins should be 0″.

SOLUTION:

As shown on page 177 of the student text. The rectangle has a solid fill, should be 1/8″ high and 4″ long, and should appear .5″ in from the left edge of this 5″ by 7″ document. The squares should be .5″ apart and should be aligned at the top of the rectangle. The company name should be 14/14.5 bold; "Attorneys-at-Law" should be 10/12, small caps. These two lines should appear .5″ in from the left edge of this 5″ by 7″ document and should be force-justified across 3″. The announcement body should appear 2″ in from the left edge of this 5″ by 7″ document. The first three lines of the announcement body should be serif 12/14 italic, double-spaced. A quadruple-space should separate the last of these lines from the first line of address information. The address information should be serif 14/16 bold, double-spaced, except for the telephone numbers, which should be normal. A quadruple-space should separate the last line of the telephone number from the date, which should be serif 12/14 italic. A shortened version of the filled rectangle, with the square centered horizontally and vertically, should appear in the two locations as shown.

LESSON 14: FORMATTING INVITATIONS AND ANNOUNCEMENTS

EXERCISE 92

DISK FILES: Students will need a symbol from a symbol typeface appropriate for an announcement by a law office of lawyers' promotions.

LEVEL: 1

LEARNING OBJECTIVES:

Format an announcement

DESKTOP TECHNIQUES APPLIED:

Use a custom page size, format text in different fonts, draw boxes with fills, change the alignment of text, choose an appropriate symbol

PREPARATION/MATERIALS:

Students will need a symbol from a symbol typeface appropriate for an announcement by a law office of lawyers' promotions.

TEACHING SUGGESTIONS:

- Go over the design pointers/hints.

- Review the following desktop techniques as appropriate and necessary: setting a custom page size and choosing symbols from symbol typefaces.

SETTINGS:

The page should be 5" by 7". All margins should be .25".

SOLUTION:

As shown on page 179 of the student text. The shading is 60% gray. The company name is 14-point bold. The text of the announcement is 12/14, small caps, except for the last two lines, which are 10-point italic (no small caps). Students may use any appropriate symbol instead of the diamonds; if a symbol typeface is unavailable, they have been instructed to create short 2-point lines instead. The address text is 10/auto bold.

LESSON 14: FORMATTING INVITATIONS AND ANNOUNCEMENTS

EXERCISE 93

DISK FILES: Students will need a graphic or symbol from a symbol typeface appropriate for an engagement announcement.

LEVEL: 1

LEARNING OBJECTIVES:

Format an announcement
Place graphic elements and adjust spacing attractively

DESKTOP TECHNIQUES APPLIED:

Use a custom page size, draw a box with rounded corners, format text in different fonts, set tracking and character width, add graphic elements to text

PREPARATION/MATERIALS:

Students will need a graphic or symbol from a symbol typeface appropriate for an engagement announcement.

TEACHING SUGGESTIONS:

■ Review the following desktop techniques as appropriate and necessary: setting a custom page size, choosing rounded corners for a box, changing the tracking of text, changing the character width of text, changing the image control settings for a graphic, placing a graphic as an inline graphic, obtaining symbols from a symbol typeface, and applying color to text and graphic elements.

SETTINGS:

The page should be 5" by 7". All margins should be .75" except the left margin, which should be 1".

SOLUTION:

As shown on page 181 of the student text. Students should have created a 1-point box border with rounded corners .25" outside the margins of the document, which has a custom size of 5" by 7". The word "joy" should be in 130-point sans serif bold, with very loose tracking and spacing set at 125%, if available. The word should be aligned at the right margin. The rest of the text should be in 9/22 serif italic. An appropriate graphic or symbol from a symbol typeface should appear at the beginning of each line of the serif text. Color and/or image control should have been used, if appropriate, to enhance the graphics. The elements should be arranged as shown.

LESSON 15: FORMATTING FLYERS

EXERCISE 94

DISK FILES: MOVE (template file)

LEVEL: 1

LEARNING OBJECTIVES:

Format a flyer

DESKTOP TECHNIQUES APPLIED:

Rotate text, format text in different fonts, add space after text, add bullets, reset tabs, draw shapes with fills

TEACHING SUGGESTIONS:

■ Review the following desktop techniques as appropriate and necessary: rotating text, setting left and right indents, adding space after text, force-justifying text, inserting desktop publishing software bullets, and resetting tabs.

SETTINGS:

The left and top margins should be 2.25"; the right and bottom margins should be .75".

SOLUTION:

As shown on page 183 of the student text. Note that the solution has been reduced. All text should be sans serif. A 1-point box should frame the margins. The rotated text should be 1/8" outside the left margin and should be flush with the bottom margin. The flyer text should have a .125" left and right indent. There should be 4.5" from the top of the page to the base of "RE-LO-CATE." That text should be 59-point. The following line should be 20-point with em spaces between the words, force-justified, and with .5" of space after. The next paragraph and the bulleted text should be 14-point. Bullets should appear 1.5" from the left margin. The text of bulleted items should appear 1.75" from the left margin. The last bulleted item should be followed by .35". The last four lines should be 18-point.

The truck should appear just inside the left and right margins as shown. The top of the trailer should begin 3/4" from the top of the page, should be 3.5" wide by 1.25" tall, should have 60% shade, and should have a 1-point line. The "R" should be in sans serif 59-point bold reverse and should be centered on the top of the trailer. The bottom of the trailer should be 3.75" wide by .25" tall. The cab should be 1" wide by 1.25" tall and should begin 1" from the top of the page and 6" from the left edge of the page. The window and door should have a 1-point line. The wheels should be .5" in diameter; the outer part of the wheels has a 1-point line and 60% shade. There should be 2.5" from the top of the page to the base of the wheels.

LESSON 15: FORMATTING FLYERS

EXERCISE 95

DISK FILES: GARDEN (template file). Students will also need two graphics suitable for a garden center flower sale.

LEVEL: 1

LEARNING OBJECTIVES:

Format a flyer
Place and size graphics attractively

DESKTOP TECHNIQUES APPLIED:

Draw a rectangle, import text and graphics files, set text in different fonts, add space after text, use the reflect option

PREPARATION/MATERIALS:

Students will need two graphics suitable for a garden center flower sale.

TEACHING SUGGESTIONS:

- Review the following desktop techniques as appropriate and necessary: setting left and right indents, adding space after text, saving a file as a template, and using the reflect option.

SETTINGS:

The left and right margins should be 2.5", the top margin should be 1", and the bottom margin should be .75".

SOLUTION:

As shown on page 185 of the student text. Note that the solution has been reduced. All text should be serif. A double-line box should frame the margins. "Green Thumb Garden Center" should be 18/17, with .35" after "Garden Center." "Announces...springtime" should be 22/20, with .75" after "springtime." "Flower Sale" should be 48/40, with .5" after "Sale." The remaining text should be 12/14, with .25" left and right indents. Text should be centered vertically between the top and bottom margins. Students should have used a graphic in the four margin corners as shown; it classroom software has a reflect option and if students judged a reflected copy to look attractive, students should have used a reflected copy in the opposite corner. The larger graphics (again, the same graphic in parallel locations) should appear between .25" in from the edge of the page and the margin. Students should size and place a graphic as they consider attractive and should use a reflected copy for the copy opposite if they considered the result pleasing.

LESSON 15: FORMATTING FLYERS

EXERCISE 96

DISK FILES: Students will need a graphic suitable for a Fourth of July sale at a furniture store.

LEVEL: 1

LEARNING OBJECTIVES:

Format a flyer

DESKTOP TECHNIQUES APPLIED:

Create a star, rotate an object and text, import a graphic file, place multiple copies of graphics, adjust the lightness of an image

PREPARATION/MATERIALS:

Students will need a graphic suitable for a Fourth of July sale at a furniture store.

TEACHING SUGGESTIONS:

- Review the following desktop techniques as appropriate and necessary: creating a polygon, creating a star, rotating objects, using multiple paste with horizontal offset, and changing the lightness of an image.

SETTINGS:

All margins should be .75".

SOLUTION:

As shown on page 187 of the student text. Note that the solution has been reduced. Students should have used a 4-point line around the margins, up to the coupons. The star should have a 2-point line; if a star feature is not available, students were instructed to create an oval. The text in the star should be 30/auto. The graphic at the right may vary, of course. Body text should begin 1" from the left margin and 3 5/8" from the top of the page and should extend to .5" short of the right margin. The first two paragraphs should be 18/24. The address information should be 14/auto. Students should have double-spaced between sections of text. The coupons should begin at 8" from the top of the page. The shaded box, which should have 60% shade and no line, should be 1/8" in on the top, left, and right of the coupon and should be .5" deep. "DOORBUSTERS" should be 24-point. The rest of the text should be 14-point. Both "DOORBUSTERS" and the following text should be aligned horizontally and vertically. The graphic should have 75% lightness and 50% contrast.

LESSON 16: FORMATTING ADVERTISEMENTS

EXERCISE 97

DISK FILES: Students will need a graphic suitable for an advertisement about movies.

LEVEL: 1

LEARNING OBJECTIVES:

> Learn advertisement format
> Format an advertisement

PREPARATION/MATERIALS:

> You may wish to bring in, or have students bring in, examples of advertisements. Students will need a graphic suitable for an advertisement about movies.

DESKTOP TECHNIQUES APPLIED:

> Set image lightness and contrast, key text in different fonts, set a left indent, draw rules and boxes with fills, use copy and paste features

TEACHING SUGGESTIONS:

- Go over the description of advertisements, referring to pages 188-189 of the student text. If you or students have brought in examples of advertisements, examine and circulate them.

- Review the following desktop techniques as appropriate and necessary: changing image control settings and setting a left indent.

SETTINGS:

> The left and right margins should be 1.875". The top and bottom margins should be 2".

SOLUTION:

> As shown on page 189 of the student text. The border should frame the margins. The baseline of the first line of text should be 2.5" from the top of the page; the text should begin 2.25" from the left edge of the page. Text should be serif 12/auto bold. Graphics will vary, of course, but should be set to 75% lightness and 50% contrast as shown. Students should have returned three times and keyed the next two lines in sans serif 14/auto bold, center-aligned, with no left indent (the rest of the text in the exercise has no left indent). Students should have keyed three returns and keyed "NOTORIOUS" in sans serif 24/auto bold, center-aligned. The next line should be serif 10/auto bold, center-aligned, and followed by two returns. The word "and" should be sans serif 14/auto bold, center-aligned. The text of "39 STEPS" should be sans serif 24/auto bold. The steps should consist of 1-point lines. Students should have arranged the completed steps attractively as in the example. The date, time, and location text should be serif 14/auto bold, center-aligned; the baseline of the first line of that text block should be 7.25" from the top of the page. Students should have returned twice after the "Admission" line. The last two lines should be sans serif 14/auto, bold, reverse, and center-aligned. The box should have a solid fill and no line.

LESSON 16: FORMATTING ADVERTISEMENTS

EXERCISE 98

DISK FILES: Students will need three graphics suitable for an advertisement about a limousine service. They will also need a symbol from a symbol typeface for a bullet.

LEVEL: 1

LEARNING OBJECTIVES:

Format an advertisement

PREPARATION/MATERIALS:

Students will need three graphics suitable for an advertisement about a limousine service. They will also need a symbol from a symbol typeface for a bullet.

DESKTOP TECHNIQUES APPLIED:

Drag to create text blocks, key text in different fonts, key text with tabs and bullets, apply color to text and graphics, set image lightness and contrast

TEACHING SUGGESTIONS:

- Review the following desktop techniques as appropriate and necessary: dragging to create a text block, setting left indents and space after text, setting tabs, applying color to text and graphics, and changing image control settings.

SETTINGS:

The left and right margins should be 1.625". The top and bottom margins should be 3.125".

SOLUTION:

As shown on page 191 of the student text. The border, which should have a 4-point line and rounded corners, should frame the margins. The graphic at the top should extend from .25" in from the left margin to .25" in from the right margin. Graphics, of course, will vary. All text should be sans serif. The title should be 18-point bold/italic, with .18" after. The second line should be 12-point bold. In both lines, en spaces should be used between words and between words and the bullet. The bullet should be a desktop publishing software bullet. Both lines should be force-justified. The telephone number should be 36-point bold, center-aligned, and red. The bulleted text should be indented .5" from the left margin, should be 11/auto, should have a tab set at approximately 2 5/8" from the left margin, and should have em spaces between bullets and the text that follows. Bullets may vary but should be red. The graphic behind the bulleted text should be set to 75% lightness and 50% contrast.

LESSON 17:   FORMATTING BROCHURES

EXERCISE 99

DISK FILES: CAREER (template file). Students will also need a symbol for a check box from a symbol typeface, if possible.

LEVEL: 2

LEARNING OBJECTIVES:

Learn brochure format; format a brochure

DESKTOP TECHNIQUES APPLIED:

Use landscape orientation, set text in columns, kern text, create a raised cap, rotate text, draw rules and boxes with fills

PREPARATION/MATERIALS:

You may wish to bring in, or have students bring in, examples of brochures.   Students will also need a symbol for a check box from a symbol typeface, if possible.

TEACHING SUGGESTIONS:

- Discuss the purpose and formatting of brochures, referring to the information on page 192 and the model on pages 193 and 195 of the student text. If you or students have brought sample brochures to class, examine and circulate them.
- Review the following desktop techniques as appropriate and necessary: setting columns, choosing the snap to guides option, creating styles, aligning text baseline to baseline, inserting space after paragraphs, kerning, using software bullets, keying en spaces, resetting tabs, obtaining a character symbol from a symbol typeface, setting left indents, rotating text.

SETTINGS:

The top and bottom margins should be .5"; the left and right margins should be 25".

SOLUTION:

As shown reduced on pages 193 and 195 of the student text. On page 1 (Panels 2, 3, and 4), body text should be 11/14. "CONFERENCE HIGHLIGHTS" text should be sans serif 13-point. Conference titles should be sans serif 12/14. Conference numbers should be sans serif 11/14. Dashed lines should sit on the top and bottom margin guides for each column (.5"). Column gutters should be .5". Text should begin .75" from the top of the page. Students should have adjusted text for violations of hyphenation rules and should have aligned it baseline to baseline at the top and bottom. On page 2 (Panels 5 and 6 and the front cover), the text in Panel 5 and on the front cover should begin .75" from the top of the page. The dashed lines in Panel 5 should sit on the top and bottom margin guides for each column (.5"). Text in Panel 5 should be serif 14/24; the raised cap should be 36-point bold. Students should have kerned the "W" and "h," if necessary, and should have checked for violations of hyphenation rules. In Panel 6, the dashed box should frame the margins, sitting, at the top and bottom, on the margin guides, like the dashed lines in Panel 5. The first three lines should be sans serif; the rest, serif. The first line should be 11/auto; the rest, 10/auto. In the first line, dates should be right-aligned. In the second, desktop publishing software bullets and en spaces should appear between items as shown. The second line should be followed by a .5-point rule; all other rules should be 1-point. Students should have added .1" after the lines beginning "Whitmore College," "Fees," "To register," "Telephone," "Enter the number," and "Signature." Students may have used another symbol for the check box; if they did not have a symbol, students should have drawn 1-point rules. The front cover is framed by a rectangle with 60% fill and no line. The rotated text should be serif 38/auto bold, 120% width. The rest of the text should be sans serif 14/auto reverse, with a 1.15" left indent, and should break line for line. The rules between parts are 8-point, should be centered vertically between text sections, should be the same length, and should be as long as the longest line of text.

LESSON 17: FORMATTING BROCHURES

EXERCISE 100

DISK FILES: COMPUTER (template file). Students will also need two graphics suitable for a brochure about a computer service store (see exercise copy on pages 197 and 199 of the student text).

LEVEL: 2

LEARNING OBJECTIVES:

Format a brochure

DESKTOP TECHNIQUES APPLIED:

Use landscape orientation, set text in columns, import text and graphics files, change the font of text, adjust the lightness of an image

PREPARATION/MATERIALS:

Students will need two graphics suitable for a brochure about a computer service store (see exercise copy on pages 197 and 199 of the student text).

TEACHING SUGGESTIONS:

■ Review the following desktop techniques as appropriate and necessary: setting columns, using a multiple paste feature with offset, aligning text and graphics using ruler guides, setting left indents, and changing the image settings of a graphic.

SETTINGS:

All margins should be 1".

SOLUTION:

As shown reduced on pages 197 and 199 of the student text. All text should be sans serif with auto leading. The text in Panel 1 on page 1 should be 10-point and should begin at the top and left margins. In Panel 2, text should begin at approximately 5 9/16" from the left edge of the page and 1.5" from the top of the page. The "4" should be 150-point; the vertical-line part of the "4" should be 6.5" from the left edge of the page. "SERVICE...INC." should be approximately 7 1/16" in from the left edge of the page and should be 34-point. The next line should be 12-point. The remainder of the text in the story should be 9-point. The four reverse lines should be aligned with "SERVICE...INC." above. The rectangles should extend from 6.5" in from the left margin to the right margin. Graphics, of course, will vary.

On page 2, all text should begin at the top margin. Column gutters should be .5". Text should be justified. Headings should be center-aligned, centered vertically within their rectangles, and aligned baseline to baseline as shown. Graphics should also be aligned. The large graphic, which will vary, should have 75% lightness and 50% contrast.

LESSON 18: FORMATTING MENUS

EXERCISE 101

DISK FILES: **SYMPH** (template file). If students have an option for grouping objects and re-sizing them as a group, they will also need **SHAPES1** (data file).

LEVEL: 2

LEARNING OBJECTIVES:

Learn about menu formatting
Format a menu

DESKTOP TECHNIQUES APPLIED:

Use landscape orientation, draw shapes with fills and rules, import a text file, set a right-aligned tab with leaders, adjust the spacing of text

PREPARATION/MATERIALS:

You may wish to bring in, or have students bring in, examples of menus.

TEACHING SUGGESTIONS:

- Discuss the purpose and formatting of menus, referring to the information on page 200 and the model on pages 201 and 203 of the student text. If you or students have brought sample menus to class, examine and circulate them.

- Review the following desktop techniques as appropriate and necessary: choosing landscape orientation, choosing the snap to guides option, setting columns, setting a right-aligned tab with leaders, inserting space after paragraphs, aligning text baseline to baseline, using a multiple paste feature with vertical offset, changing the measurement system of the vertical ruler to picas, grouping objects, and re-sizing objects as a group.

SETTINGS:

All margins should be .5".

SOLUTION:

As shown reduced on pages 201 and 203 of the student text. On page 1, the large rectangle should extend to the top, left, and bottom margins; its right border should be 7" from the left edge of the page. The black keys should be .25" tall and 2" wide. They should begin at these positions from the top of the page: 1", 1 3/4", 3 1/4", 4", 4 3/4", 6 1/4", and 7". The shorter lines framing the white keys should be 1-point and should extend from the midpoint of the black keys to the right margin. The two longer lines framing the white keys should extend from the large rectangle to the right margin and should be 2 5/8" and 5 5/8" from the top of the page. The text should be serif 12-point bold and reverse, should be right-aligned, should be centered in the three keys as shown, and should end as shown slightly short of the end of the keys.

On page 2, the gutter should be .167". Text should begin at the top margin and should extend the full width of each 4 7/8" column. Text should be serif 10/15. Prices should be right-aligned with leaders as shown. Two courses should appear in Column 1 and three in Column 2 as shown. The first and last lines of the columns should align baseline to baseline, and students should have inserted space so that the columns end evenly as shown. The scales should consist of hairline rules about 3 points apart, should extend the width of the column, and should be centered between each course title and the first food item as shown.

LESSON 18: FORMATTING MENUS

EXERCISE 102

DISK FILES: **PALM** (template file). Students will also need a graphic that complements the restaurant title ("The Palm Cafe").

LEVEL: 1

LEARNING OBJECTIVES:

Format a menu

DESKTOP TECHNIQUES APPLIED:

Import text and graphics files, use em spaces and en spaces, force-justify text, create a style based on text, draw a filled box

PREPARATION/MATERIALS:

Students will need a graphic that complements the restaurant title ("The Palm Cafe").

TEACHING SUGGESTIONS:

- Go over the design pointers/hints.

- Step 10 calls for students to insert a small measured amount of space between letters in the course headings. A thin space or the equivalent on classroom software would be appropriate. If a thin space or the equivalent is not available, students can skip this part of Step 10.

- Review the following desktop techniques as appropriate and necessary: creating em spaces and en spaces, force-justifying text, formatting text with paragraph rules, and creating a style based on text.

SETTINGS:

All margins should be .5".

SOLUTION:

As shown on page 205 of the student text. Note that the solution has been reduced. Graphics, of course, will vary; they should appear above the word "PALM." The restaurant title should be sans serif 14-point. The course headings should be sans serif 10-point. The rules should be .5-point and should extend to the left and right only as far as the longest menu item ("Vanilla Ice Cream with Hot Chocolate Mousse - $4.00"). The remainder of the text should be serif 9/18 italic. If a thin space or the equivalent is available, students should have inserted it between each pair of letters in each course heading. An em space plus an en space should appear between "$2.50" and "Tea" and "$2.50" and "Soft Drinks."

LESSON 18: FORMATTING MENUS

● **EXERCISE 103**

DISK FILES: SUNSET (template file). Students will also need a graphic with a desert or Southwest theme.

LEVEL: 1

LEARNING OBJECTIVES:

Format a menu

DESKTOP TECHNIQUES APPLIED:

Drag-place a text file, reset a tab, draw rules and shapes with fills, use copy and paste features, import and re-size graphics

PREPARATION/MATERIALS:

Students will need a graphic with a desert or Southwest theme.

TEACHING SUGGESTIONS:

■ Review the following desktop techniques as appropriate and necessary: drag-placing a text file, resetting tabs, and using a multiple paste feature with offset.

SETTINGS:

All margins should be .5".

SOLUTION:

As shown on page 207 of the student text. Note that the solution has been reduced. Graphics, of course, will vary; they should appear as shown. The rectangle should be just inside the top, left, and right margins and should be .5" deep. The first three rules below the rectangle should be 1/8" apart; the next two should be .25" apart; and the last two should be .5" apart. The weight of the rules should be, in order, 4-point, 2-point, 1-point (two lines), .5-point, and hairline (two lines). Text should begin just under 2.5" from the top of the page and 2.25" from the left edge of the page. The second column of text should be 4.75" from the left edge of the page. The title should be 14/auto; the rest of the text should be 9/auto. The dotted rules should appear 2" and 4.5" from the left edge of the page, should begin flush with the first food item, and should end at the bottom margin.

LESSON 19: FORMATTING NEWSLETTERS

EXERCISE 104

DISK FILES: CONEWS (template file). Students will also need two graphics files, one relating to sports and the other a clock or another office graphic (see page 209 of the student text).

LEVEL: 1

LEARNING OBJECTIVES:

Learn newsletter format
Format a newsletter

DESKTOP TECHNIQUES APPLIED:

Set up columns, draw rules and boxes with fills, import text and graphics files, change the font of text, adjust the spacing of text

PREPARATION/MATERIALS:

You may wish to bring in, or have students bring in, examples of newsletters. Students will need two graphics files, one relating to sports and the other a clock or another office graphic (see page 209 of the student text).

TEACHING SUGGESTIONS:

- Discuss the purpose, formatting, and parts of newsletters, referring to pages 208 and 209 of the student text. If you or students have brought sample newsletters to class, examine and circulate them.

- Review the following desktop techniques as appropriate and necessary: setting up columns, drag-pasting text, adding space after text, using text wrap, aligning text baseline to baseline, and inserting a graphic as an inline graphic.

SETTINGS:

The left and right margins should be .75". The top margin should be 2.5". The bottom margin should be 1".

SOLUTION:

As shown on page 209 of the student text. Note that the solution has been reduced. Graphics, of course, will vary; they should appear as shown. The two horizontal rules should be 1-point, should extend from margin to margin, and should appear at 1" and 2.25" from the top of the page. The date, which should be 15/auto with very loose tracking, should appear just above the rule at 1". The box enclosing it should be 40% gray with no line. "JOB TALK" should be 55/auto with very loose tracking. The next line should be 18/auto; the first five words should be in small caps. That line should appear slightly above the horizontal rule at 2.25".

The text of the newsletter should begin 2.5" from the top of the page. Body text should be 12/13; headings should be 14/14. A .5-point rule at 4.25" from the left edge of the page should appear between the columns. The rule should extend from the top to the bottom margin. The gutter should be .167". The first and last lines should be aligned baseline to baseline across columns. The two columns should end evenly.

LESSON 19:   FORMATTING NEWSLETTERS

EXERCISE 105

DISK FILES: ALUMNI (template file). Students will also need a graphic appropriate for an alumni newsletter

LEVEL: 2

LEARNING OBJECTIVES:

Format a newsletter

DESKTOP TECHNIQUES APPLIED:

Draw rules and boxes with fills, import text and graphics files, drag-paste text, set tracking and character width, adjust the spacing of text

PREPARATION/MATERIALS:

Students will need a graphic appropriate for an alumni newsletter

TEACHING SUGGESTIONS:

- Review the following desktop techniques as appropriate and necessary: setting up columns, drag-pasting text, changing tracking and character width, adding space after text, and aligning text.

SETTINGS:

All margins should be .75".

SOLUTION:

As shown on pages 211 and 213 of the student text. Note that the solution has been reduced. On page 1, the rule at the top should be 6-point and should extend across the top margin and from the left to the right margin. "WESTLAKE CLUB" should be 45-point; its baseline should be 1.5" from the top of the page. The next line should be 18-point; the first three words should have very loose tracking and 130% width. That line should be slightly above the box. The box should be 2" from the top of the page, should begin approximately 2.25" from the left edge of the page, and should be 2" square. The line extending from it should go to the left margin. Both should be 6-point. Graphics, of course, will vary. The calendar should begin 4 3/8" from the top of the page. The title and dates should be 14/auto; the other text should be 12/auto. The material after the dates should be indented 1.5". The box at the bottom of the column should have a 1-point rule and 10% shade. It should end even with the baseline of the last line of text in the right column. The boxed text should be 10/auto. The rest of the text in the newsletter should be 12/auto. The text in Column 2 should begin 2.5" from the top of the page.

On page 2, the box, graphic, and rule from page 1 should appear at the top margin. The box should be approximately 4 5/16" in from the left edge of the page (the box will be partly in the gutter). The rule should extend to the left margin as shown. Text in the first column should begin 2" from the top of the page. Text in the second column should begin approximately 3.5" from the top of the page. The last lines of the columns should align baseline to baseline.

LESSON 19: FORMATTING NEWSLETTERS

EXERCISE 106

DISK FILES: VITAMIN (template file). Students will also need three graphics files relating to healthy food and a symbol from a symbol typeface for a bullet.

LEVEL: 2

LEARNING OBJECTIVES:

Format a newsletter

DESKTOP TECHNIQUES APPLIED:

Set up columns, import text and graphics files, drag-paste text, set tracking and character width, adjust the spacing of text

PREPARATION/MATERIALS:

Students will need three graphics files relating to healthy food and a symbol from a symbol typeface for a bullet.

TEACHING SUGGESTIONS:

- Review the following desktop techniques as appropriate and necessary: setting up columns, drag-pasting text, changing tracking and character width, aligning text baseline to baseline, adding space after text, setting hanging and right indents, and creating styles.

SETTINGS:

The left and top margins should be 1". The right margin should be .75". The bottom margin should be 1.25".

SOLUTION:

As shown on pages 215 and 217 of the student text. Note that the solution has been reduced on page 215. The gutter should be .167". Graphics, of course, will vary. On page 1, the baseline of "HEALTHWATCH" should be approximately 2" from the top of the page; the text should begin approximately 3 3/8" from the left edge of the page. "HEALTH" should be sans serif 55-point, with 70% width and very loose track. "WATCH" should be sans serif 38-point, with 120% width and tight track. The line under the text should be 12-point. The text beneath the line should be sans serif 12-point, with 80% width and very loose track. The text in columns on page 1 should begin 3" from the top of the page. The "In This Issue" text should be sans serif 12/12, with 90% width and 1-point rules above and below. The two articles on page 1 should be serif 10/11. Text in Column 1 should end 8.5" from the top of the page. Text in Columns 2 and 3 should end 7" from the top of the page. The first and last lines of those columns should be aligned baseline to baseline, and the columns should end evenly as shown. The "Tips" text should begin 7" from the top of the page. The heading should be sans serif 12/13. The rest of the text should be sans serif 9/11 with a hanging indent so that the bullet is at .125" and the text to the right of the bullet is at .375". The text should have a right indent of .125" and .05" after paragraphs. Students may have used another symbol or a drawn object for the bullet.

On page 2, "EATING FOR ENERGY" should be sans serif 24/32, with very loose track and 110% width. Its baseline should be 2" from the top of the page. The line below it should be 2-point. The three subheadings should be sans serif 14/14. The body text should be 12/12, justified. The columnar text should begin at 2.25" from the top of the page and the subheadings should be aligned baseline to baseline. The dashed line should appear 5.5" from the top of the page. "HEALTH" should be sans serif 40-point, with 70% width and loose track. "WATCH" should be sans serif 35-point, with 120% width and tight track. The line below the title should be 6-point. The rest of the return address should be sans serif 10/12, with 90% width and very loose track. The postmark data should be sans serif 9/12, with 90% width and very tight track.

LESSON 20: PUBLISHING ELECTRONICALLY

EXERCISE 107

DISK FILES: VITAMINS (data file)

LEVEL: 1

LEARNING OBJECTIVES:

Learn formatting guidelines for electronic publishing
Convert a document to electronic format

PREPARATION/MATERIALS:

In this exercise, students will convert a previously prepared desktop-published file to electronic format. It is strongly recommended that the instructor work through the exercise before class to ensure that it will proceed smoothly for students.

The exercise is written for PageMaker 6.0 Windows with Adobe Acrobat. Two components of Adobe Acrobat available on the PageMaker 6.0 CD-ROM, Acrobat Distiller and Acrobat Reader (or the equivalent applications for classroom equipment), must be installed before students can complete the exercise.

Since directions for exercise steps may differ significantly across programs, you may wish to work through this exercise with your students as a class.

TEACHING SUGGESTIONS:

- Discuss the preparation of documents for electronic distribution, referring to page 218 of the student text.

- Emphasize issues of compatibility across computers and browser applications. Make sure students understand when a "published" format is desirable and when it is impractical, unworkable, or unnecessary.

SOLUTION:

Students should have opened their PDF or equivalent file in their viewer application. The file should have looked quite similar to the **VITAMINS** document they prepared in Exercise 106. Students should then have printed a copy of the document from their viewer application, not from their desktop publishing software. The printed copy should look quite similar to the solution on pages 215 and 217 of the student text. For details about the solution, see page 114 of this manual.

LESSON 20: PUBLISHING ELECTRONICALLY

EXERCISE 108

DISK FILES: PF (template file)

LEVEL: 1

LEARNING OBJECTIVES:

Learn formatting guidelines for the World Wide Web
Create and format a document for Web distribution

DESKTOP TECHNIQUES APPLIED:

Format text with styles

PREPARATION/MATERIALS:

In this exercise, students will create and format a document for Web distribution. If your school has a Web server account or home page, you may wish to have students actually publish this document or another document on the Web.

In the exercise, students create a hypertext link to an anchor within the document. If your school has a Web server account or home page, you may wish to have students create links to each other's documents or to the home page.

Since directions for exercise steps may differ significantly across programs, you may wish to work through this exercise with your students as a class.

TEACHING SUGGESTIONS:

- Discuss the preparation of documents for distribution on the Web, referring to page 220 of the student text.

- Make sure students understand that much of the formatting ordinarily applied to desktop-published documents is not supported by Web browsers. Students should use the standard HTML styles for formatting text.

- This exercise is written for PageMaker 6.0 Windows with the HTML Author plug-in. Remind students to substitute the appropriate steps for their software.

SOLUTION:

As shown on page 221 of the student text. Note that the solution has been reduced. Text should be in the default serif typeface for your system (Times New Roman, for example). The title should be 24/auto bold. Body text should be 12/auto. The two headings should be 18/auto. The first should be bold; the second should be underscored and in a different color.

LESSON 21: FORMATTING PRESENTATION GRAPHICS

EXERCISE 109

DISK FILES: Students will need two symbols from a symbol typeface or graphics. See page 222 of the student text.

LEVEL: 1

LEARNING OBJECTIVES:

Learn presentation graphics format
Format presentation graphics

PREPARATION/MATERIALS:

Students will need two symbols from a symbol typeface or graphics. See page 222 of the student text.

DESKTOP TECHNIQUES APPLIED:

Use landscape orientation, set elements on a master page, key text in different fonts, use graphic symbols, replace text with new text

TEACHING SUGGESTIONS:

- Define a **presentation graphic.** Go over the guidelines for producing presentation graphics, referring to pages 222-223 of the student text.

- Review the following desktop techniques as appropriate and necessary: setting items on a master page, setting left indents and space after text, creating a star with the polygon tool, and obtaining symbols from a symbol typeface.

SETTINGS:

All margins should be 1".

SOLUTION:

As shown on page 223 of the student text. Note that the solution has been reduced. The border should frame the margins. The baseline of the logo should be 1.75" from the top of the page; the logo should begin 1.25" from the left edge of the page. Symbols may vary. Text should be sans serif 24/auto bold. On the sales meeting graphic, the baseline of the title should be 3" from the top of the page. On the selling points graphic, the baseline of the title should be 3.5" from the top of the page. On both pages, title text should be 36/auto sans serif bold, center-aligned, with .25" after. On both pages, enumerated/bulleted text should be 24/auto sans serif bold, left-aligned, with .25" after, numbers/bullets appearing 3" from the left edge of the page, and the text that follows 4" from the left edge of the page. For the selling points page, students may have used a different bullet.

LESSON 21: FORMATTING PRESENTATION GRAPHICS

EXERCISE 110

DISK FILES: **STARR** (data file)

LEVEL: 1

LEARNING OBJECTIVES:

Format a presentation graphic

DESKTOP TECHNIQUES APPLIED:

Replace text with new text, add a page to a document, create a pie or bar chart

TEACHING SUGGESTIONS:

■ Review the following desktop techniques as appropriate and necessary: inserting a page in a document and creating a pie or bar chart. Pages 136-139 of the student text may be of help.

SETTINGS:

All margins should be 1".

SOLUTION:

As shown on page 225 of the student text. Note that the solution has been reduced. The border should frame the margins. The baseline of the title should be 2.75" from the top of the page. The title should be 36/auto sans serif bold, center-aligned, with .12" after. The subtitle should be 30/auto sans serif bold, center-aligned. Students should have created and placed attractively a bar or pie chart using the information on the chart on page 225.

ON-YOUR-OWN PROJECTS: SAMPLE SOLUTIONS

Students are given very little direction in how to complete these projects; thus, solutions will vary widely. For Exercises 111 and 112, students should create their own personal resume and letterhead. Exercise 113 should have the same measurements and text as in the example, which is shown full-size. Exercise 114 should measure 5" by 7" and should have the same text as the example. Exercise 115 should have the same text as the sample. Exercise 116 should have 2 pages with 3 panels per page; the text should match that of the example. Exercise 117 should measure 5" by 7" and should have the same text as in the sample. Exercise 118 should have the same text as the example. For Exercise 119, text will vary, since students write it. Exercises 120-125 should have the same text as the examples. Titles for Exercise 122 will vary. Most solutions are shown reduced.

EXERCISE 111

Alice Fox
519 Gwynne Allen Estates Drive • Apartment 1A
Catskill, NY 12414-4545 • (518) 555-6453 (home) • (518) 555-3761 (work)

EDUCATION

University of Kentucky: M.A., Mass Communication, 1993
B.A., Telecommunications, 1991

WORK EXPERIENCE

Associate Professor   Department of Communications

1997-Present
Green County Community College • Catskill, New York

Teach *Basic Public Speaking* and *Introduction to Interpersonal Communication*, as well as *Newswriting Practicum*. Instruct classes both on-campus and at off-campus extension. Reestablished student newspaper and act as faculty advisor.

Instructor

1997-Present
Basic Skills and Employability • Catskill, New York

Designed and teach 40-hour workshop on *Interpersonal Communication Skills/Life Skills Management* for economically disadvantaged persons.

Developmental Editor

1993-1997
Athena Publishing Co. • Lexington, Massachusetts

Worked with authors to write manuscripts of language arts multimedia products. Hired, managed, and coordinated outside contractors for varied editorial services. Developed a dozen projects simultaneously. Traveled to sales conferences and spoke about new products.

Teaching and Research Assistant   Department of Telecommunications

1989-1991
University of Kentucky • Lexington, Kentucky

Taught *Introduction to Mass Media* in discussion labs and served as Lab Assistant for *Television Production* course. Developed lectures, designed tests, and graded research papers. Grader for introductory and upper-level Telecommunications courses.

REFERENCES

References available upon request.

EXERCISE 112

Alice Fox
519 Gwynne Allen Estates Drive • Apartment 1A
Catskill, NY 12414-4545 • (518) 555-6453 (home) • (518) 555-3761 (work)

EXERCISE 113

Appletree
Books

❧ Books, music, and software
❧ Rare books a specialty

14 Gilchrist Street ❧ San Francisco, CA
94102-4483

Telephone: 800-555-2468
FAX: 415-555-0010
http://wwx.grand.net/applbks

EXERCISE 114

Marivel and Raymond Malagos

announce the engagement

of their daughter

Josephine

to

Michael Ramos

son of

Maria and Roberto Ramos

December 21, 19--

EXERCISE 115

The New York City
Jazz Festival

What better way to spend spring...visiting New York City...and listening to jazz bands from all over the country. For seven nights, you can listen to performances of:

The Rider International Drums Competiton
The Quincy Adams Big Band
The Lincoln Center Orchestra (tunes from the jazz-band era)

May 1-8, 19--

For complete ticket information, call 212-555-3333.
The New York City Jazz Festival is sponsored by the Eye-On-New York Association.

EXERCISE 116 (page 1 of 2)

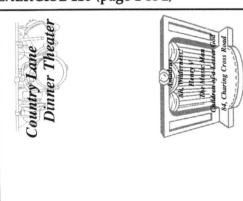

Country Lane Dinner Theater

Amadeus
Ah, Wilderness!
Henry V
The Music Man
Children of a Lesser God

84, Charing Cross Road

Summer Schedule

Country Lane Dinner Theater
345 Spring Road
Orlando, FL 32809-6767

SENSATIONAL SHOWS

The Country Lane Dinner Theater summer schedule includes six award-winning shows. If you like an intricate detective story, thought-provoking drama, and the music of Mozart, come to see *Amadeus*. For comedy and nostalgia, Eugene O'Neill's *Ah, Wilderness!* is the ticket. Lovers of musicals can thrill to the well-loved standard *The Music Man*. Do you like Shakespeare? Our production of *Henry V* follows the standard set by Kenneth Branagh. We round out the season with the thought-provoking *Children of a Lesser God* and Helene Hanff's warm and witty *84, Charing Cross Road*.

SENSATIONAL DINNERS

The best shows deserve the best meals to accompany them. The Country Lane Dinner Theater offers a substantial menu, including prime rib, pork roast, surf 'n turf, and our famous Bottomless Buffet. This season we've added some choice vegetarian entrees to our menu selections. After you've dined in style, settle down with some gourmet coffee and a sumptuous dessert, and enjoy the show!

SENSATIONAL EVENINGS

At the Country Lane Dinner Theater, your pleasure and comfort are our number-one concern. Air conditioning, plush seats, solicitous attendants, and first-class service are our standard. Please let us know how we can make your theater-going and dining experience as satisfying as possible.

EXERCISE 116 (page 2 of 2)

Summer Schedule

June 1-14   *Amadeus*

Peter Shaffer's heart-stopping drama about the musical genius Wolfgang Amadeus Mozart and his envious rival Antonio Salieri. Did Salieri murder Mozart, or not?

June 15-28   *Ah, Wilderness!*

In this warm comedy set in the innocent America of 1906, renowned playwright Eugene O'Neill sketches a compelling portrait of innocence, family relationships, and first love.

June 29-July 12   *Henry V*

William Shakespeare's patriotic portrait of the famous young king in his manhood and the decisive battle of Agincourt.

July 13-August 2   *The Music Man*

Meredith Wilson's beloved musical story of Professor Harold Hill, a traveling, flimflamming seller of boys' bands, his journey to River City, Iowa, and his encounter with the town librarian, Marian Paroo.

August 3-16   *Children of a Lesser God*

Mark Medoff's masterful play about a teacher of deaf children and the deaf woman with whom he falls in love.

August 17-30   *84, Charing Cross Road*

The warm and true story of the friendship in letters of Helene Hanff, a struggling writer in New York, and Frank Doel, a London bookseller.

Pricing and Policies

The Country Lane Dinner Theater offers one show each evening at 7:30 p.m. with a 6:00 p.m. dinner seating and a Saturday matinee at 2:00 p.m. with a 12:00 noon luncheon seating. Reservations are required and may be made by telephoning (407) 555-8282.

TICKETS

Mon. - Thurs.	$20.00
Fri. & Sat. Evening	$25.00
Saturday Matinee	$18.00

Any two shows:	$5.00 discount
All six shows:	$25.00 discount

• Ticket prices do not include dinner.
• All major credit cards accepted.
• Patrons arriving after the opening of a show will be seated at the first convenient break in the play's action.
• Smoking is not permitted in the theater.
• All tables are wheelchair-accessible.

Call now for your reservation for award-winning dramas and musicals and sumptuous dinners
The Country Lane Dinner Theater
555-8282

Menu

APPETIZERS

Chicken Wings	$3.95
Cheese and Fruit Plate	$4.95
Seafood Sampler	$5.95
Soup of the Day	$2.95

ENTREES

Prime Rib	$18.00
Filet Mignon	$18.95
New York Strip	$20.00
Pork Roast	$18.95
Alaska Crab	$25.00
Blackened Halibut	$25.00
Surf 'n Turf	$25.00
Pasta with Red Sauce	$12.95
Vegetarian Lasagna	$12.95
Bottomless Buffet	$15.00

All entrees except our Bottomless Buffet are served with a basket of fresh, homemade rolls; a light salad; your choice of potato or rice; and two vegetables (brussels sprouts, broccoli, carrots, corn, spinach, or Swiss chard).

DESSERTS

Boston Cheesecake	$3.50
Key Lime Pie	$3.50
Apple Torte	$2.95
Zucchini Spice Cake	$4.95
Biscuit Sampler	

BEVERAGES

Soft Drinks	$1.00
Milk	$1.00
Juice	$1.00
Coffee	$1.50
Cafe au Lait	$2.25
Cafe Mocha	$2.25
Espresso	$1.95

ON-YOUR-OWN PROJECTS: SAMPLE SOLUTIONS

EXERCISE 117

The Blue Skies Society

invites you

on a tour of ten historic houses

of Walnut Hills

Saturday, December 17

12 p.m. - 7 p.m.

Reception to follow

at Spicer House

Proceeds to benefit

Kids First

Tickets: $50.00

R.S.V.P. by December 10

Ms. June Alford

555-1432

EXERCISE 118

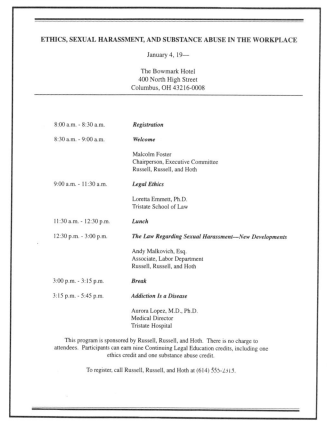

Party Bonanza

15 McGee Avenue
Berkeley, CA 94703-2280
(415) 555-8200

EXERCISE 119

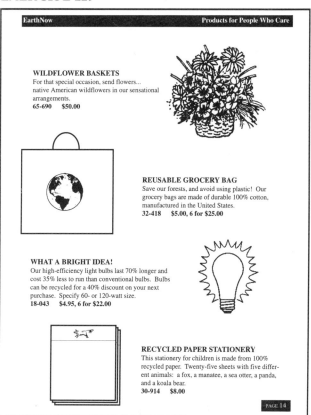

EarthNow   **Products for People Who Care**

WILDFLOWER BASKETS
For that special occasion, send flowers...
native American wildflowers in our sensational
arrangements.
65-690 $50.00

REUSABLE GROCERY BAG
Save our forests, and avoid using plastic! Our
grocery bags are made of durable 100% cotton,
manufactured in the United States.
32-418 $5.00, 6 for $25.00

WHAT A BRIGHT IDEA!
Our high-efficiency light bulbs last 70% longer and
cost 35% less to run than conventional bulbs. Bulbs
can be recycled for a 40% discount on your next
purchase. Specify 60- or 120-watt size.
18-043 $4.95, 6 for $22.00

RECYCLED PAPER STATIONERY
This stationery for children is made from 100%
recycled paper. Twenty-five sheets with five different animals: a fox, a manatee, a sea otter, a panda,
and a koala bear.
30-914 $8.00

PAGE 14

EXERCISE 120

ETHICS, SEXUAL HARASSMENT, AND SUBSTANCE ABUSE IN THE WORKPLACE

January 4, 19—

The Bowmark Hotel
400 North High Street
Columbus, OH 43216-0008

8:00 a.m. - 8:30 a.m.	*Registration*
8:30 a.m. - 9:00 a.m.	*Welcome*
	Malcolm Foster
	Chairperson, Executive Committee
	Russell, Russell, and Hoth
9:00 a.m. - 11:30 a.m.	*Legal Ethics*
	Loretta Emmett, Ph.D.
	Tristate School of Law
11:30 a.m. - 12:30 p.m.	*Lunch*
12:30 p.m. - 3:00 p.m.	*The Law Regarding Sexual Harassment—New Developments*
	Andy Malkovich, Esq.
	Associate, Labor Department
	Russell, Russell, and Hoth
3:00 p.m. - 3:15 p.m.	*Break*
3:15 p.m. - 5:45 p.m.	*Addiction Is a Disease*
	Aurora Lopez, M.D., Ph.D.
	Medical Director
	Tristate Hospital

This program is sponsored by Russell, Russell, and Hoth. There is no charge to
attendees. Participants can earn nine Continuing Legal Education credits, including one
ethics credit and one substance abuse credit.

To register, call Russell, Russell, and Hoth at (614) 555-2315.

EXERCISE 121

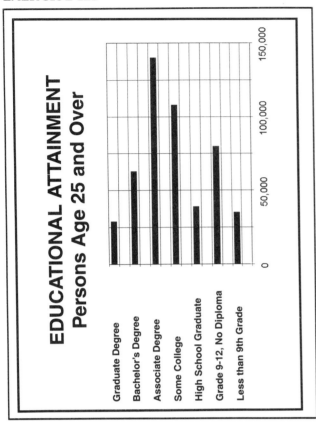

EDUCATIONAL ATTAINMENT
Persons Age 25 and Over

- Graduate Degree
- Bachelor's Degree
- Associate Degree
- Some College
- High School Graduate
- Grade 9-12, No Diploma
- Less than 9th Grade

(0, 50,000, 100,000, 150,000)

EXERCISE 122 (page 1 of 3)

Restoring Old Neighborhoods:
A Plan for Prosperity

Carapace
June 14, 19--

EXERCISE 122 (page 2 of 3)

RESTORING OLD NEIGHBORHOODS:
A PLAN FOR PROSPERITY

Six blocks from James Ortez's apartment in Smythville is a block of fine old houses dating from the 1700s. These once-stately buildings carry an imposing history. Ship captains, merchants, and statesmen once lived there. Their builders included Nicholson Conant, a leader in the Revolutionary War, and Abigail Wainwright, a noted poet. Considered architectural landmarks in their day, these buildings have been worn by time and neglect to a jumble of dilapidated structures that are a neighborhood eyesore and a scene of drug deals and other crime.

Five blocks from Rose Feeley's apartment in Jonestown is a block of fine old houses dating from the 1700s. Once run-down and empty like those in Smythville, these houses have been meticulously restored to their former grandeur. Consisting of some shops, homes reserved for tourism, and private homes, they have been designated National Historic Sites and are visited frequently on many regional tours. This neighborhood in Jonestown has experienced a 35 percent increase in property values, a 45 percent reduction in crime, and a 15 percent rise in employment directly attributable to the rehabilitation of these old homes. (Willis, 1996, 14)

Smythville and Jonestown are typical of some 1,500 communities up and down the Eastern seaboard whose fortunes have been, or are capable of being, transformed by the restoration of neglected historic properties. In a recent study of 200 communities with similar rehabilitation projects, increases in property values only five years after restoration ranged from 15 to 60 percent; reduction in crime, from 20 to 73 percent; and rise in employment, from 8 to 39 percent. (Penobscot, 1997, 34) Here in our own state, some 153 communities are seeking funds for restoration projects with the potential of bringing infusions of money and jobs, reducing crime, improving neighborhoods, and raising property values: improving the lives of some 6,120,000 citizens.

The mission of Carapace is to restore historic homes in old neighborhoods to their former state. A nonprofit organization, Carapace has been in operation for some 25 years. In that time, we have restored 729 Colonial houses in 57 communities. Our work has been praised by architects for its faithfulness to the architecture of original structures and by community planning boards for its cost-effectiveness. A major architectural publication recently stated, "Carapace's restoration of the Ambrose mansion is perhaps the most significant and successful restoration of a Colonial home in the past five years." (Chang, 1998, 12) Three years after the restoration of a block of houses in Waynesville, the mayor said, "Carapace's work has brought new life into the Arbor neighborhood. I would unhesitatingly recommend them to any community seeking to restore fine old homes and improve the livelihood of citizens." (Ortez, 1997, 3)

In collaboration with 25 communities in our state, Carapace is seeking a grant of $53,000,000 for 25 neighborhood restoration projects to be completed over a period of ten years. Our plan is to

EXERCISE 123 (page 3 of 3)

2

draw on our considerable past experience to develop and implement a streamlined method of rehabilitating old homes that will be both architecturally faithful and cost-effective. After our plan has been developed and successfully tried in these 25 restoration projects, we shall make it available to the other 128 communities in our state currently considering restoration, and to communities in other states as well.

A general breakdown of the time frame and estimated spending for this project follows:

CARAPACE PROJECT
Time Frame and Estimated Spending

Initial Planning	.5 yrs.	$ 250,000
Communities A-F	2.5 yrs.	$13,125,000
Communities G-L	2 yrs.	$13,125,000
Communities M-R	2.5 yrs.	$13,125,000
Communities S-Y	2 yrs.	$13,125,000
Review and Refinement	.5 yrs.	$ 250,000
Total Direct Costs		**$53,000,000**

Restoration of historic homes can be a risky proposition. Lack of communication, disagreement about the importance of architectural integrity versus costs, and other factors can derail projects or significantly escalate their costs. With a tested plan by an agency with 25 years of experience and a solid track record among both architects and communities, the restoration of fine old homes, the revitalization of their communities, and improvement of the lives of citizens, can proceed in a steady, assured manner.

REFERENCES

Celia Chang. "Recent Colonial Restorations." *Architectural News*, Spring 1998, 10-18.

John Ortez. "The Arbor—Old Homes, New Life." *Waynesville Daily News*, January 14, 1997, 3.

Diana Penobscot. "The Good Statistics of Rehabilitation." *Community Journal*, Summer 1997, 32-38.

Fred Willis. "The Rising Fortunes of Jonestown." *Tristate Courier,* September 4, 1996, 14.

EXERCISE 123 (page 1 of 2)

A Quarterly Publication of the Kona Club   March 19--

ENVIRONMENT
NEWS

Inside

Save the Forests   1

Plants Are Our Friends   1

Four Tips To Help the Environment 1

Animal in the News:
THE CUCKOO BIRD   2

Club News and Events   2

SAVE THE FORESTS

In parts of the United States, particularly the Pacific Northwest, trees are disappearing. The Forest Watch Wilderness Program trains volunteers to work with the United States Forest Service to protect the nation's forests.   For more information, write to:

Attention: Director, National Forest Program
The Wilderness Society
900 Seventeenth Street
Washington, DC 20006

PLANTS ARE OUR FRIENDS

NASA researchers have found that certain household plants, when placed where air circulates, actually remove harmful indoor air pollutants that cause eye and throat irritation. Plants such as the spider plant and peace lily are inexpensive, easy to find, and a great gift for an allergy sufferer. For a list of "friendly" plants, call Greenery Solutions at 1-718-553-3555.

FOUR TIPS TO HELP THE ENVIRONMENT
by Neely Larson

1.   *Walk, Walk, Walk!* Walk on errands instead of driving. Walking not only is good exercise but also reduces air pollution caused by gasoline. Walk to the grocery store, the drugstore, the playground, or the library. When you are going shopping, park in a central location and walk to your different stops.

2.   *Use Containers, Not Wrap or Foil.* Containers can be used instead of plastic wrap, plastic bags, or foil to store any type of food. Choose sturdy containers with a tight seal that are microwave- and freezer-safe. Buy a variety of sizes for different uses.

3.   *Have an Eco-Friendly Lawn.* Avoid striving for a lawn of pure grass. Certain plants such as clover and even weeds are beneficial to lawns, as they help break up the soil. Many fertilizers and lawn chemicals are harmful to children and pets and contaminate groundwater.

EXERCISE 123 (page 2 of 2)

Page 2

ENVIRONMENT
NEWS

4.   *Recycle Scrap Paper.* Always use both sides of a piece of paper before recycling it. If your community does not support recycling of computer paper, consider donating it to schools, which often welcome extra paper for student crafts. Or start computer paper recycling in your community!

ANIMAL IN THE NEWS: THE CUCKOO BIRD

The cuckoo, known for its clear, repetitive two-note call, has a very unusual nesting ritual. Once a cuckoo's eggs have been fertilized, the female prepares for her main task of depositing the eggs in the nests of other birds. The female cuckoo lands on a nest of another bird and lays a single egg in that nest. She then removes one of the host bird's eggs from the nest and flies away. Sometimes the host bird detects the switch and will abandon its nest and build another one. The cuckoo is persistent, however, and will try to deposit her eggs in the re-made nest. In fact, newly hatched cuckoo chicks show an innate urge to eject all other eggs out of their nest. Using its strong stumpy wings, the cuckoo chick lifts the eggs or other chicks of the host bird onto its back, up to the edge of the nest, and throws out!

CLUB NEWS AND EVENTS

The next meeting of the Kona Club will be on April 24 at 6:30 p.m. A light dinner will be served. For reservations, call Janet Halvorsen at 415-555-9736.

EXERCISE 124

PATTISON SCHOOL LATCHKEY PROGRAM REGISTRATION

Child's name _____ Date _____
Address _____
City _____ State _____ ZIP _____
Birth date _____ Home phone _____ Present grade _____

Registering for:

	P.M.	P.M. drop-in
Monday	☐	☐
Tuesday	☐	☐
Wednesday	☐	☐
Thursday	☐	☐
Friday	☐	☐

Father: Name _____
Place of employment: _____ Position: _____
Address: _____ Business phone: _____
Hours of employment: _____

Mother: Name _____
Place of employment: _____ Position: _____
Address: _____ Business phone: _____
Hours of employment: _____

Please list two people to contact in an emergency if a parent cannot be reached:

1. Name:_____ Relationship to child: _____
    Phone number (during latchkey hours): _____

2. Name: _____ Relationship to child: _____
    Phone number (during latchkey hours): _____

Please list any pertinent health information: _____
_____
_____

I fully understand that should my child(ren) be accepted into the Pattison School Latchkey Program, my registra- tion fee of $10, which I submitted for admission to Pattison School Latchkey Program, is non-refundable under any circumstances, before or after the program starts.
Signature _____ Date _____

I give my permission for the Pattison School Latchkey Director and Staff to view pertinent health and school records concerning my child(ren).
Signature _____ Date _____

EXERCISE 125

THE BAEDEKER FUND		
STATEMENT OF CHANGES IN NET ASSETS		

	Year Ended December 31, 19—	Six Months Ended June 30, 19—
INCREASE IN NET ASSETS		
Operations:		
Net Investment Income	$ 85,173	$ 49,114
Realized Net Gain on Investment Securities Sold Based on Identified Cost	52,868	40,102
Change in Unrealized Appreciation of Investment Securities	129,195	125,539
Net Increase in Net Assets Resulting from Operations	267,236	214,755
DISTRIBUTIONS:		
Net Investment Income	(85,546)	(73,733)
Realized Net Gain	(11,948)	(52,836)
Total Distributions	(97,494)	(126,569)
NET EQUALIZATION CREDITS	365	993
CAPITAL SHARE TRANSACTIONS:		
Issued —Regular	161,276	158,018
—In Lieu of Cash Distributions	70,586	97,024
—Exchange	125,940	66,078
Redeemed —Regular	(144,964)	(76,932)
—Exchange	(129,314)	(70,367)
Net Increase from Capital Share Transactions	83,524	173,821
Total Increase	253,631	263,000
NET ASSETS		
Beginning of Period	1,273,706	1,527,337
End of Period	$1,527,337	$1,790,337
(1) Distributions Per Share		
Net Investment Income	$.98	$.78
Realized Net Gain	$.14	$.58
(2) Shares Issued and Redeemed		
Issued	18,099	13,440
Issued in Lieu of Cash Distributions	4,544	5,981
Redeemed	(17,189)	(8,854)
	5,454	10,567
(3) Undistributed Net Investment Income	$36,032	$12,406
Paid in Capital	$1,240,133	$1,413,954

JOB 1 (page 1 of 4)

The Downtown Glover Shopping Gazette
Volume X, Number X

Date, 19--

AN ARTICLE CAN GO HERE

This is practice or "dummy" text that you can use for importing, placing, and playing purposes. Desktop publishers often use dummy text. When you are first designing a publication, you can flow a dummy text file in to see how your design will look with type. Desktop publishers also use dummy text for publications that will be produced periodically, such as a monthly newsletter. The dummy text serves as a placeholder

for the different articles that will appear in each issue. You will learn more about using dummy text in this way in later exercises.

Some desktop publishing programs give you practice or "dummy" text that looks like Latin (but it's not). It is called a *lorem ipsum* file. Really, any file can serve as dummy text. The more it looks like the kind of text you will be using in your final publication,

the better. You can manipulate and move sections of practice text as you desire. You can experiment with different elements such as typefaces, type styles, type sizes, and leading.

Later in this book, you will be given the opportunity to create your own projects. Before you tackle them, you will learn to plan your publication ahead by drawing a "thumbnail" sketch on a piece of blank paper. Drawing a thumbnail will give you direction in creating your page layout on the computer. The sketch should define the approximate positions of all the text and graphic elements that will appear on each page. Of course, the design may be changed as you are working on your project in the desktop publishing program.

There are countless ways to design a document. Professional designing requires education and skill, but you do not have to be a professional designer to create simple, attractive publications in your desktop publishing software. The exercises in this book will give you the general guidelines you need for document design, as well as ideas to consider

AN ARTICLE CAN GO HERE

This is practice or "dummy" text that you can use for importing, placing, and playing purposes. Desktop publishers often use

The Downtown Glover Shopping Gazette is a publication of the Glover Visitors Bureau, 14 Cabot Street, Glover, MA 01915-4459, telephone (508) 555-2000.

Editor: Norma McRae
Publications Assistant: Your Name

dummy text. When you are first designing a publication, you can flow a dummy text file in to see how your design will look with type. Desktop publishers also use dummy text for publications that will be produced periodically, such as a monthly newsletter. The dummy text serves as a placeholder for the different articles that will appear in each issue. You will learn more about using dummy text in this way in later exercises.

Some desktop publishing programs give you practice or "dummy" text that looks like Latin (but it's not). It is called a lorem ipsum file. Really, any file can serve as dummy text. The more it looks like the kind of text you will be using in your final publication, the better. You can manipulate and move sections of practice text as you desire. You can experiment with different elements such as typefaces, type styles, type sizes, and leading.

JOB 1 (page 2 of 4)

2

Bed-and-Breakfast News

This is practice or "dummy" text that you can use for importing, placing, and playing purposes. Desktop publishers often use dummy text. When you are first designing a publication, you can flow a dummy text file in to see how your design will look with type. Desktop publishers also use dummy text for publications that will be produced periodically, such as a monthly newsletter. The dummy text serves as a placeholder for the different articles that will appear in each issue. You will learn more about using dummy text in this way in later exercises.

Some desktop publishing programs give you practice or "dummy" text that looks like Latin (but it's not). It is called a lorem ipsum file. Really, any file

BAND SHELL BANTER

This is practice or "dummy" text that you can use for importing, placing, and playing purposes. Desktop publishers often use dummy text. When you are first designing a publication, you can flow a dummy text file in to see how your design will look with type. Desktop publishers also use dummy text for publications that

will be produced periodically, such as a monthly newsletter. The dummy text serves as a placeholder for the different articles that will appear in each issue. You will learn more about using dummy text in this way in later exercises.

Some desktop publishing programs give you practice or "dummy" text that looks like Latin (but it's not). It is called a lorem ipsum file. Really, any file can serve as dummy text. The more it looks like the kind of text

JOB 1 (page 3 of 4)

3

The Itinerant Gourmet

This is practice or "dummy" text that you can use for importing, placing, and playing purposes. Desktop publishers often use dummy text. When you are first designing a publication, you can flow a dummy text file in to see how your design will look with type. Desktop publishers also use dummy text for publications that will be produced periodically, such as a monthly newsletter. The dummy text serves as a placeholder for the different articles that will appear in each issue. You will learn more about using dummy text in this way in later exercises.

Some desktop publishing programs give you practice or "dummy" text that looks like Latin (but it's not). It is called a lorem ipsum file. Really, any file can serve as dummy text. The more it looks like the kind of text you will be using in your final publication, the better. You can manipulate and move sections of practice text as you desire. You can experiment with different elements such as typefaces, type styles, type sizes, and leading.

This is practice or "dummy" text that you can use for importing,

placing, and playing purposes. Desktop publishers often use dummy text. When you are first designing a publication, you can flow a dummy text file in to see how your design will look with type. Desktop publishers also use dummy text for publications that will be produced periodically, such as a monthly newsletter. The dummy text serves as a place

This is practice or "dummy" text that you can use for importing, placing, and playing purposes. Desktop publishers often use dummy text. When you are first designing a publication, you can flow a dummy text file in to see how your design will look with type. Desktop publishers also use dummy text for publications that will be produced periodically, such as a monthly newsletter. The dummy text serves as a placeholder for the different articles that will appear in each issue. You will learn more about using dummy text in this way in later exercises.

Some desktop publishing programs give you practice or "dummy" text that looks like Latin (but it's not). It is called a lorem ipsum file. Really, any file can serve as dummy text. The more it looks like the kind of text you will be using in your final publication, the better. You can manipulate and move sections of practice text as you desire. You can experiment with different elements such as typefaces, type styles, type sizes, and leading.

This is practice or "dummy" text that you can use for importing, placing, and playing purposes. Desktop publishers often use dummy text. When you are first designing a publication, you can flow a dummy text file in to see

JOB 1 (page 4 of 4)

4

Another Article Goes Here

This is practice or "dummy" text that you can use for importing, placing, and playing purposes. Desktop publishers often use dummy text. When you are first designing a publication, you can flow a dummy text file in to see This is practice or "dummy" text that you can use for importing, placing, and playing purposes. Desktop publishers often use dummy text. When you are first designing a publication, you can flow a dummy text file in to see This is practice or "dummy" text that you can use for importing, placing, and playing purposes. Desktop publishers often use dummy text. When you are first designing a publication, you can flow a dummy text file in to see This is practice or "dummy" text

that you can use for importing, placing, and playing purposes. Desktop publishers often use dummy text. When you are first designing a publication, you can flow a dummy text file in to see
This is practice or "dummy" text that you can use for importing, placing, and playing purposes. Desktop publishers often use dummy

Glover Visitors Bureau
14 Cabot Street
Glover, MA 01915-4459

Bulk Rate
U.S. Postage
Paid
Glover, Mass.
Permit No. 7580

For notes on solutions, see page 132.

GLOVER, MASSACHUSETTS, VISITORS BUREAU (SIMULATION): SAMPLE SOLUTIONS

JOB 2 (page 1 of 4)

The Downtown Glover Shopping Gazette
Volume 1, Number 1   June 1-15, 19--

VISITORS BUREAU OFFERS HISTORIC TOURS

The Glover Visitors Bureau, at 14 Cabot Street in downtown Glover (555-2000), offers tours of historic Glover for all needs and interests. You can choose from bus and walking tours, a children's tour, a garden tour, and tours for senior citizens.

Each tour visits three historic homes. **The Foxx house** was the home of James Foxx, a well-to-do merchant in the China trade in the 1700s. The

house contains many of the original furnishings. On display is Captain Foxx's collection of Chinese pottery. **Bancroft House** was the home of Eliza Bancroft, the poet and member of the Transcendentalist movement. Some or her original manuscripts are on display. **Abbott Gardens,** which dates from 1750, was the home of George Abbott, the famous statesman and delegate to the First Continental Congress, and his influential wife,

Alma. The house is surrounded by a breathtaking garden.

Each tour takes visitors by the **sea wall,** where marks of cannonballs remind us of how British forces attacked the town in the Revolutionary War. We pass several old sea captains' homes, with their picturesque widow's walks and quiet gardens. Weekend tours stop at the home of **Nathaniel Westcott,** captain of one of the first ships of the American navy, under the command of General George Washington.

We also visit the **First Baptist Church,** which dates to 1675. The church is noted for its fine architecture and old graveyard. A special memorial has been built to **The Reverend Joshua Wycott,** an influential figure in the Abolitionist movement and the Underground Railroad.

No tour is complete without a stop at **Pickett Park.** Adults can walk in the quiet gardens or repose in the sun, while children collect shells, play in the sand, and enjoy the playgrounds.

Metamorphosis
18 Cabot Street
Glover, MA 01915-4459
555-1303

New and lightly used fashions
Locally made jewelry
New Age cassettes and CDs
Cosmetics and body products
Environmentally responsible and cruelty-free

Free apple balm sunblock stick with this ad
Expires 6/15/--

THE MAGIC CARPET TAKES CHILDREN ON A SPECIAL RIDE

The Magic Carpet, located at 24 Rantoul Street, offers a fine selection of traditional and new children's books for you and your

child to enjoy. From Alice Applebaum to Harry Zadar, the Magic Carpet brings you the work of the finest children's authors, in editions to fit any budget. They also offer a selection of acclaimed children's software and a special collection of science

discovery books for every age. The Magic Carpet features a comfortable reading area, where you and your child can sit down and read any book you are considering before purchase.

The Magic Carpet
24 Rantoul Street
Glover, MA 01915-2314
555-9232

The Downtown Glover Shopping Gazette is a publication of the Glover Visitors Bureau, 14 Cabot Street, Glover, MA 01915-4459, telephone (508) 555-2000.

Editor: Norma McRae
Publications Assistant: Your Name

JOB 2 (page 2 of 4)

2

Findlay Fruit and Vegetable Market
56 Cabot Street
Glover, MA 01915-4459 • 555-0935

Locally grown in summertime...
the best produce all year 'round.
• Fruit baskets a specialty.
• Free local delivery.

$1 worth of produce free with a $2 purchase
Expires 6/15/--

BAND SHELL BANTER

The music of Mozart and the sounds of the big-band era will be offered during the next two weekends in the **Band Shell Concerts** at Pickett Park. From six to eight in the evening, bring a blanket or lawn chairs and a picnic dinner, and settle down for good music and plenty of fun.

June 6-8, listeners can enjoy the **Glover Community Orchestra**

rendering some of Mozart's most popular works. Selections from *The Magic Flute, Don Giovanni,* and *The Marriage of Figaro* will be offered, as well as *Piano Concerto No. 15 in B flat* and *Piano Concerto No. 21 in C.*

June 13-15, **The Marty Moreno Big Band** will entertain us with the music of Glenn Miller, Benny Goodman, and other favorite artists of the big band era. Find a partner and swing along to *Moonlight Serenade, String of Pearls, Take the 'A' Train,* and *In the Mood.*

Marvel's Pharmacy

PHARMACY & HOME MEDICAL EQUIPMENT

Free Delivery
24-Hour Emergency Service

Senior Citizens Discount

Insurance Plans Accepted

Credit Cards Accepted

Personal Service at Discount Prices!

18 Rantoul Street
555-1400

Bed-and-Breakfast News

Hancock House, at 37 Beach Street, is a fine old Colonial home overlooking the sea. Built in 1793 by a Glover merchant, the house features fine mahogany and cherry woodwork, period furnishings, a patterned garden, and a well-stocked library.

Owners Stephanie and Robert Foster have painstakingly restored the house. They are well-informed about its history and are delighted to take their guests on a tour, including the widow's walk and a secret staircase to a cellar where valuables were stored. They can recommend sites to visit and make reservations at local restaurants.

Hancock House features seven well-appointed single and double rooms—three with views of the sea—and two shared baths. A continental breakfast is offered. Reservations are recommended, particularly in the summer (555-9427).

Amity Pottery
9 Rantoul Street
Glover, MA 01915-2314
555-9120

Hand-crafted

http://wwx.grand.net/amity

The Depot Coffee Shop

Stop in anytime....
for gourmet coffee,
fresh-brewed tea,
homemade doughnuts,
strudel, and other delights.

Open 6 a.m. - 11 p.m.

Free cup of coffee or tea with this ad

At the train station
94 Bridge Street • Glover, MA 01915-2243 • 555-1240

JOB 2 (page 3 of 4)

3

The Itinerant Gourmet

This week the Itinerant Gourmet visited **Annie's Corner Cafe,** located at 13 Front Street. In business for five years, Annie's serves lunch and dinner in a comfortable and quietly elegant atmosphere.

I began with the cheese and fruit plate, a selection of delectable Vermont cheeses and summer fruits. Other appetizers included chicken wings, hors d'oeuvres, and jumbo shrimp.

The lunch and dinner menu features a variety of gourmet pizzas and sandwiches as well as pasta dishes, fresh fish, and chicken. Several vegetarian entrees are offered.

For my entree, I enjoyed Annie's Favorite Pasta, linguine in a light cheese sauce, delicately flavored with herbs. Served with a generous, fresh-made salad and rolls baked on the premises, it was more than an ample meal and very reasonably priced at $8.95. With my meal, I had a glass of iced tea, flavored with mint and lemon and replenished free of charge.

The dessert menu features a variety of baked goods, including apple pie, cherry pie, carrot cake, chocolate walnut cake with vanilla frosting, bread pudding, an assortment of cookies, and several flavors of ice cream. I ordered Apple Pie A La

Mode, which was served piping hot and topped with a scoop of vanilla ice cream. With my pie, I had the house decaffeinated coffee, a rich and mellow blend.

From start to finish, my meal was absolutely delicious. Prompt, courteous service and unobtrusive music contributed to my dining pleasure.

Lena's Ice Cream
9 Dane Street
"By-the-beach"

Homemade
Ice Cream
25 flavors
Sundaes
Banana splits
Milkshakes
Frappes

Free single-dip cone with this ad!
Expires June 15, 19--

Open 11 a.m. - 11 p.m.

Wildlife Explorer Opens to Nationwide Acclaim

Wildlife Explorer is a critically acclaimed documentary of endangered species. Produced by noted wildlife expert Cody Thomas, *Wildlife Explorer* is showing by special engagement June 1 to June 15 at the **Hester Street Cinema.**

Cody Thomas has studied and fought for endangered species for the past 30 years. Now he brings his knowledge and his message before the public in this film of animals all around the world.

Thomas unflinchingly documents the devastation wreaked by humankind for profit and pleasure on the habitats and existence of once-prominent species. He chronicles the effects of pesticides, water pollution, oil spills, strip mining, drainage of swamps, and leveling of forests on animal species. He also examines the trapping and killing of wild animals for their pelts or other body parts.

Just as meticulously, Thomas records for us the lives of these animals when undisturbed by human incursions. He renews an often-made plea that responsible citizens make themselves the caretakers of other species and take appropriate measures to stop exploitation and abuse.

The Hester Street Cinema is located at 24 Hester Street in downtown Glover. A public parking lot is available across the street. Showings are at 2, 5, and 8 p.m. daily, with an additional showing at 11 a.m. on weekends.

The Ryder Bike Shop
18 Front Street, Glover, MA 01915-8234   555-7832

Selling and renting bicycles for all users. Racing bikes, all-terrain vehicles, children's cycles, popular name brands.

1 Hour Free Rental with purchase of 2 hours
Expires 6/15/--

JOB 2 (page 4 of 4)

4

Spotlight on... Gordon's Department Store

Thinking of living in Glover?

We can help!

Corey & Brown Realtors

555-9345

34 Cabot Street
Glover, MA 01915-4459

Gordon's Department Store, downtown at 43 Cabot Street, has been a Glover particular for 30 years. Prompt, friendly, and courteous service is a Gordon tradition. The salesclerks are never in too much of a hurry to help you choose just the right scarf or tie, to call around to other stores if an item is not in stock, or simply to pass the time of day. Gordon's offers men's, women's, and children's wear; large domestics and appliances departments; jewelry and cosmetics; toys; fine china; candy; and yarn, crafts materials, and fabric goods. Children and adults alike go to Gordon's for slow-roasted cashews and peanuts, locally made divinity, and fresh-popped popcorn, the pleasant smell of which pervades the second floor. Instead of canned music with high-pressure commercials every five minutes, Gordon's plays for its customers WGUM, the local classical music station. Gordon's once-a-month Crazy Day sale is the place for unlooked-for bargains in every department. Coats from a factory outlet in Swampscott and children's clothing from an outlet in Falmouth are always good buys. The store sponsors a scholarship at Glover High School and regularly supports local school, church, and community events. Gordon's offers a senior citizens discount Tuesdays and Fridays.

*The **Glover Visitors Bureau** is ready to help you with reservations, directions, and advice. Give us a call at 555-2000, or stop by our offices in downtown Glover, at 14 Cabot Street.*

Glover Visitors Bureau
14 Cabot Street
Glover, MA 01915-4459

Bulk Rate
U.S. Postage
Paid
Glover, Mass.
Permit No. 7580

For notes on solutions, see page 132.

JOB 3

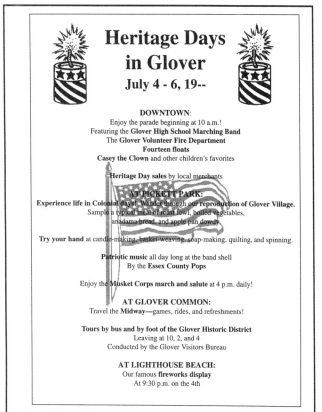

Heritage Days in Glover
July 4 - 6, 19--

DOWNTOWN:
Enjoy the parade beginning at 10 a.m.!
Featuring the **Glover High School Marching Band**
The **Glover Volunteer Fire Department**
Fourteen floats
Casey the Clown and other children's favorites

Heritage Day sales by local merchants

AT PICKETT PARK:
Experience life in Colonial days! Wander through our reproduction of Glover Village.
Sample a typical meal of roast fowl, boiled vegetables,
anadama bread, and apple pan dowdy.

Try your hand at candle-making, basket-weaving, soap-making, quilting, and spinning.

Patriotic music all day long at the band shell
By the **Essex County Pops**

Enjoy the **Musket Corps march and salute** at 4 p.m. daily!

AT GLOVER COMMON:
Travel the **Midway**—games, rides, and refreshments!

Tours by bus and by foot of the Glover Historic District
Leaving at 10, 2, and 4
Conducted by the Glover Visitors Bureau

AT LIGHTHOUSE BEACH:
Our famous **fireworks display**
At 9:30 p.m. on the 4th

JOB 4 (page 1 of 2)

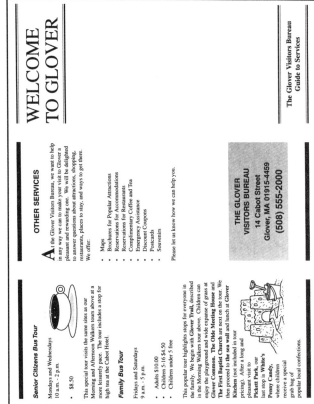

The Glover Visitors Bureau
Guide to Services

WELCOME TO GLOVER

OTHER SERVICES

At the Glover Visitors Bureau, we want to help in any way we can to make your visit to Glover a pleasant and rewarding one. We will be delighted to answer questions about attractions, shopping, restaurants, places to stay, and ways to get there. We offer:

- Maps
- Brochures for Popular Attractions
- Reservations for Accommodations
- Reservations for Restaurants
- Complimentary Coffee and Tea
- Emergency Assistance
- Discount Coupons
- Postcards
- Souvenirs

Please let us know how we can help you.

**THE GLOVER
VISITORS BUREAU
14 Cabot Street
Glover, MA 01915-4459
(508) 555-2000**

Senior Citizens Bus Tour
Mondays and Wednesdays
10 a.m. - 2 p.m.
- $8.50

This special tour visits the same sites as our Morning and Afternoon Walkers tours above at a more leisurely pace. The tour includes a stop for high tea at the Cabot Hotel.

Family Bus Tour
Fridays and Saturdays
9 a.m. - 5 p.m.
- Adults $10.00
- Children 5-16 $4.50
- Children under 5 free

This popular tour highlights stops for everyone in the family. We begin with **Glover Trail**, described above. Children can enjoy the playground and wide expanse of grass at **Glover Common**. **The Olde Meeting House** and **The First Baptist Church** are next on the tour. We then proceed to the sea wall and lunch at **Glover Kitchen** (not included in tour pricing). After a long and pleasant visit to **Pickett Park**, our last stop is **White's Penny Candy**, where children receive a special grab bag of popular local confections.

JOB 4 (page 2 of 2)

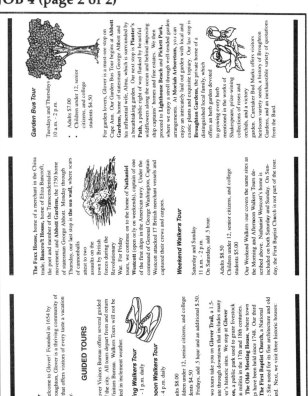

Garden Bus Tour
Tuesdays and Thursdays,
10 a.m. - 2 p.m.
- Adults $7.00
- Children under 12, senior citizens, and college students $4.50

For garden lovers, Glover is a must-see stop on Cape Ann. Our Garden Bus Tour begins at **Abbott Gardens**, home of statesman George Abbott and his influential wife, Alma, which is surrounded by a breathtaking garden. Our next stop is **Planter's Path**, a public right of way flanked by beautiful wildflowers along the ocean and behind imposing ship captains' homes and fine estates. We then proceed to **Lighthouse Beach** and **Pickett Park**, where we enjoy a stroll through well-tended garden arrangements. At **Moriah Arboretum**, you can enjoy an intricately laid out garden with local and exotic plants and exquisite topiary. Our last stop is **Broughton Gardens**, the private home of a distinguished local family, which offers an herb garden devoted to growing every herb mentioned in the works of Shakespeare, prize-winning collections of roses and orchids, and a victory garden. Caretaker Bud Marks offers visitors heirloom variety seeds, a history of Broughton Gardens, and an inexhaustible variety of quotations from the Bard.

The Foxx House, home of a merchant in the China trade; **Bancroft House**, home of Eliza Bancroft, the poet and member of the Transcendentalist movement; and **Abbott Gardens**, the 1750 home of statesman George Abbott. Monday through Thursday, our last stop is the **sea wall**, where scars of cannonballs attest to two assaults on the town by British forces during the Revolutionary War. For Friday tours, we continue on to the home of **Nathaniel Westcott** (open only on weekends), captain of one of the first ships in the American navy. Under the command of General George Washington, Captain Westcott attacked 17 British merchant vessels and captured their crews and cargoes.

Weekend Walkers Tour
Saturday and Sunday
11 a.m. - 2 p.m.
On Saturday, add .5 hour.
- Adults $8.50
- Children under 12, senior citizens, and college students $5.00

Our Weekend Walkers tour covers the same sites as the Morning and Afternoon Walkers Tours described above. Nathaniel Westcott's home is included on both Saturday and Sunday. On Sunday, the First Baptist Church is not part of the tour.

GUIDED TOURS

Welcome to Glover! Founded in 1654 by John Broughton, Glover is a thriving community of 36,000 that offers visitors a vacation to enjoy.

The Glover Visitors Bureau offers several guided tours of the city. All tours depart from and return to the Visitors Bureau. Walkers Tours will not be conducted in inclement weather.

Morning Walkers Tour
10 a.m. - 1 p.m. daily

Afternoon Walkers Tour
1 p.m. - 4 p.m. daily
- Adults $8.00
- Children under 12, senior citizens, and college students $4.50
- On Fridays, add .5 hour and an additional $.50.

These two tours take you on **Glover Trail**, a 1.5-mile route through downtown that includes many of Glover's historic sites. We stop at **Glover Common**, a public park used to graze livestock and train militia in the 17th and 18th centuries. Next is **The Olde Meeting House**, where town meetings have been held since 1748. Our third stop is **The First Baptist Church**, a National Historic Site noted for its fine architecture and old graveyard. Next, we visit three historic houses:

JOB 5 (page 1 of 18)

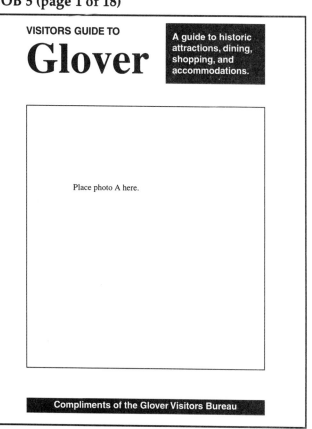

VISITORS GUIDE TO

Glover

A guide to historic attractions, dining, shopping, and accommodations.

Place photo A here.

Compliments of the Glover Visitors Bureau

For notes on solutions, see page 132.

GLOVER, MASSACHUSETTS, VISITORS BUREAU (SIMULATION): SAMPLE SOLUTIONS

JOB 5 (page 2 of 18)

CONTENTS

Welcome to Glover 2
Getting Around Glover 2
The Visitors Bureau 3
Banks/ATMS 3
Emergency Numbers 3
Shopping in Glover 4
Walking the Glover Trail 6
Away from Downtown 9
Movies and Music 10
Children's Attractions 11
Accommodations 12
Restaurants 13
Glover Summer Calendar of Events 15

WELCOME TO GLOVER

Welcome to Glover, Massachusetts, a town rich in history, with pristine beaches, pleasant shopping, beautiful architecture, outstanding restaurants, and excellent accommodations—a place for pleasure and learning. Settled in 1654 by John Broughton, Glover is a thriving community of 36,000, offering you exciting activities centered around three hundred years of history. Glover has something to offer people of all ages and tastes.

GETTING AROUND GLOVER

Unlike many early settlements, Glover is laid out on a grid pattern, making getting around easy. With the map and walking tour in this guide (see map on page 7), you can follow the Glover Trail, designated by distinctive blue signs. This trail includes 1.5 miles of sites of interest that include a memorial to a famed Abolitionist and member of the Underground Railroad; our sea wall, scarred with the marks of battle from the Revolutionary War; magnificent colonial homes; a favorite museum; and convenient restaurants, stores, and accommodations.

Place Photo B here.

2

JOB 5 (page 3 of 18)

For the driver, Glover offers several public lots conveniently located near major attractions. If you would like to leave the driving to us, the Visitors Bureau provides several different bus tours of the area. Public transportation by bus is efficient and inexpensive.

If you wish to expand your visit to other towns, Glover offers both bus and train service to Boston and surrounding communities. For bus service, call 555-2945 or 1-800-555-9231. For train information, call 555-6777 or 1-800-555-0021.

THE VISITORS BUREAU

The Glover Visitors Bureau wants to make your visit to Glover a happy and rewarding one. We are located in the heart of downtown Glover at 14 Cabot Street. Our hours are Monday through Sunday, 9 a.m. to 5 p.m. Stop by the Visitors Bureau, and let us help you plan your day. We offer guided tours by foot and bus, as well as free maps and brochures of attractions in Glover and the surrounding area.

BANKS/ATMS

These banks participate in automated teller/electronic cash network systems.

Glover Savings Bank
12 Cabot Street   555-1049

Glover Savings and Loan
14 Front Street   555-7876

EMERGENCY NUMBERS

Police (Glover) 555-0000
Fire (Glover) 555-0123
Ambulance 555-0231
Glover Hospital 555-8000
State Police 555-0001
Poison Information Center 1-800-555-9200

3

JOB 5 (page 4 of 18)

SHOPPING IN GLOVER

Downtown Glover offers shoppers an eclectic mix of thriving small businesses, some decades old, some brand-new. The following are only a few of the stops you can make on your shopping excursion.

Rantoul Street

Amity Pottery, at 9 Rantoul Street, features hand-crafted bowls, vases, tiles, and other objects.

Need a prescription refilled? At 18 Rantoul Street, **Marvel's Pharmacy** offers personal service at discount prices. Call Marvel's at 555-1400 for 24-hour emergency service and free delivery.

The Magic Carpet, located at 24 Rantoul Street, offers a fine selection of traditional and new children's books for you and your child to enjoy. The Magic Carpet features a comfortable reading area, where you and your child can sit down and read any book you are considering before purchase.

Cabot Street

Stop by **Cabot Cottage,** at 2 Cabot Street, for greeting cards, flowers and plants, and antiques and collectibles.

Across the street, at 9 Cabot Street, try **Kingdom Toys** for unique and educational toys for the youngsters on your shopping list. Kingdom Toys offers a large supervised play area.

At 28 Cabot Street, **Hannah Sisters Florists** offers floral arrangements, plants, and gift baskets for all occasions. Free delivery in Glover.

A Glover particular for 30 years, **Gordon's Department Store** at 43 Cabot Street offers men's, women's and children's wear; large domestics and appliances departments; jewelry and cosmetics; toys; fine china; candy; and yarn, crafts materials, and fabric goods. Try Gordon's for prompt, friendly, and courteous service. Their slow-roasted cashews and peanuts, locally made divinity, and fresh-popped popcorn are a treat!

Place Photo C here.

4

JOB 5 (page 5 of 18)

Located at 56 Cabot Street, the **Findlay Fruit and Vegetable Market** is the place to go for locally grown fruit and vegetables and quick, personal service. For special occasions, Findlay's fruit baskets are a Glover tradition. Findlay offers free local delivery.

Metamorphosis offers new and lightly used fashions, locally made jewelry, New Age cassettes and CDs, cosmetics, and body products. All products sold at Metamorphosis are environmentallly responsible and cruelty-free.

Dane Street

The Minuteman, at 2 Dane Street, offers locally made crafts, including pottery, wreaths, dried flower arrangements, painted ornaments, stained glass window hangings, candles, and baskets. While you are browsing, take time to admire the architecture of this beautifully restored 1810 home.

Across the street at 3 Dane Street, **Pride's Pantry** has been a Glover tradition for 69 years. This family-owned confectionery sells mouth-watering chocolates and candies of every description, attractively packaged and shipped all over the country. Try their butter mints or almond bark!

Located at 10 Dane Street, **Laurie's Antiques** features antique jewelry, furniture, sterling and silver-plated ware, lamps, pictures, china, and glass pottery.

Place Photo D here.

Wyman's Yarn and Craft Shoppe, at 14 Dane Street, offers yarn at discount prices. Wyman's features a large assortment of lace and craft supplies.

Front Street

A new bookstore in a fine old warehouse, **An Idle Hour,** at 6 Front Street, offers books, magazines, and software for every age and every taste. Quiet music, comfortable reading areas, and helpful clerks combine to make your shopping experience a pleasant one.

Ron's Factory Outlet, at 9 Front Street, gives shoppers discounts of up to 75 percent on quality name-brand clothing. Sweaters, shirts, casual and dress pants, shorts, and ties are only some of the items always on special at Ron's.

5

For notes on solutions, see page 132.

JOB 5 (page 6 of 18)

Located at 18 Front Street, the **Ryder Bike Shop** sells and rents bicycles for all users. Ryder's is the place for racing bikes, all-terrain vehicles, children's cycles, and popular name brands.

When you are visiting the **Glover Museum** at 34 Front Street, do not forget to stop into its gift shop. Here you can gifts suitable for every taste, including books, jewelry, stationery, games, crafts, science kits, rocks, arrowheads, and shells.

WALKING THE GLOVER TRAIL

Take a stroll through history on the Glover Trail, a 1.5-mile tour that includes many of Glover's historic sites and other attractions. Shops and restaurants along the way provide a convenient respite for the traveler.

1   Begin your tour at **Glover Common,** a 12-acre public park and playground bordered by Cabot, Front, and Rantoul Streets. The Common was used to graze livestock and train militia in the 17th and 18th centuries. The fine old houses around the Common were built by merchants who prospered in the China trade.

2   At 16 Cabot Street, you will find **The Olde Meeting House.** Built in 1748, the Olde Meeting House has been the site of town meetings since that time. Here, irate citizens condemned British repression and decided to join other communities in rebellion against the British Empire. Mon.-Sun., 9-5. 555-9217. Free.

3   **The First Baptist Church,** at 18 Cabot Street, dates to 1675. A National Historic Site, the church is noted for its fine architecture and old graveyard. A special memorial has been built to The Reverend Joshua Wycott, an influential figure in the Abolitionist movement and the Underground Railroad. Mon.-Sat., 9-5. Free.

Place Photo E here.

4   **The Foxx House** at 45 Cabot Street was the home of James Foxx, a well-to-do merchant in the China trade in the 1700s. The house contains

6

JOB 5 (page 7 of 18)

Please insert map of Glover trail.

Map of Glover Trail

7

JOB 5 (page 8 of 18)

many of the original furnishings. On display is Captain Foxx's collection of Chinese pottery.
Mon.-Sun., 9-5. 555-1111. Adults $1.50; children $.75; included free in Visitors Bureau tours.

5   Turning left onto Front Street, you will find at Number 8 **Bancroft House,** the home of Eliza Bancroft, the poet and member of the Transcendentalist movement. Some of her original manuscripts are on display. Mon.-Sun., 9-5. 555-6932. Adults $1.50; children $.75; included free in Visitors Bureau tours.

Place Photo F here.

6   At 11 Front Street, **Abbott Gardens,** which dates from 1750, was the home of George Abbott, the famous statesman and delegate to the First Continental Congress, and his influential wife, Alma. The house, which is a National Historic Site, is surrounded by a breathtaking garden. Mon.-Sun., 9-5. 555-2275. Adults $1.50; children $.75; included free in Visitors Bureau tours.

7   **The Glover Museum** at 34 Front Street offers an expansive collection of objects from the region's history. Native American artifacts, relics from pioneer settlements, portraits, and a fine display of Chinese pottery are among its treasures. In one room, you can walk through a replica of Glover Village, including a typical home, general store, and schoolroom. Museum volunteers in period costumes assume the roles of ship captain, printer, goodwife, and farmer. The Museum offers many hands-on, children-friendly exhibits, including Playthings from the Past, toys enjoyed through the ages by American youngsters.

Place Photo G here.

8

JOB 5 (page 9 of 18)

Mon.-Sun., 9-5. 555-0440. Adults $6.00; children 5-16 $4.00; children under 5 free; senior citizens and college students $3.

8   Traveling down two blocks and turning left on Beach Street, you will come quickly to the **sea wall.** Here marks from cannonballs attest to two assaults on the town by British forces during the Revolutionary War. The sea wall is a registered National Historic Site.

Place Photo H here.

9   At 25 Beach Street, the home of **Nathaniel Westcott** is open on the weekends. Westcott was captain of one of the first ships of the American navy, under the command of General George Washington. During the Revolutionary War, Westcott attacked 17 British merchant ships and captured their crews and cargoes. Westcott's house is a National Historic Site.
Fri.-Sun., 10-5. 555-4323. Adults $1.50; children $.75; included free in Visitors Bureau tours.

AWAY FROM DOWNTOWN

Your tour of historic Glover continues on Beach Street. You can drive this long, meandering road, which follows the coast, admiring the homes and the breathtaking view of the sea. Or, you can walk or jog along **Planter's Path,** a public right-of-way that runs behind the imposing homes of ship captains and the fine estates of later residents. The Path wanders through wildflowers, with sudden turns onto rocky vistas where you can enjoy a rest and a view of a magnificent sunset over the ocean. Either way, be sure to stop at our two public beaches, **Lighthouse Beach** and **Pickett Park.** You can stroll along cobblestone walkways in the quiet gardens, admiring the beautiful native flowers, or repose in the sun. Children can collect shells, play in the sand, and enjoy the

Place Photo I here.

9

For notes on solutions, see page 132.

GLOVER, MASSACHUSETTS, VISITORS BUREAU (SIMULATION): SAMPLE SOLUTIONS

JOB 5 (page 10 of 18)

playground. Both beaches offer cookout grills and picnic benches. If you are visiting Pickett Park on a summer weekend evening, bring a blanket or lawn chairs and a picnic dinner and stop by the band shell for an evening of musical enjoyment on the shore.

Kevin's Marina, at 45 Beach Street, and the **Glover Harbor Marina,** at 54 Beach Street, rent sailboats and rowboats by the hour. Guided motorboat tours of the area are also available at Glover Harbor.

For garden lovers, Glover is a must-see stop on Cape Ann. Besides the beautiful flowers at Pickett Park, Planter's Path, Lighthouse Beach, and historic houses, Glover offers two other large gardens.

At 14 Ascott Street **Moriah Arboretum,** founded by the China merchant and public benefactor Abner Moriah in 1825, is an intricately laid out garden with local and exotic plants, exquisite topiary, and brick paths. Mon.-Sun., 9-5. 555-1660. Free (donations are welcome).

At 9 Overlook Avenue, **Broughton Gardens,** the private gardens of an old local family, include quiet streams, wishing wells, an herb garden devoted to growing every herb mentioned in the works of Shakespeare, prize-winning collections of roses and orchids, and a victory garden. Mon.-Fri., 11-4. 555-1804.

Place Photo J here.

MOVIES AND MUSIC

The **Glover Opera Company,** in the Ascott Theatre at 24 Ascott Street, is an amateur community company of five years' standing that has received favorable notice in the Boston papers. This summer, the Company will be performing Gilbert and Sullivan's *The Mikado* and Mozart's *The Magic Flute.* Join in the fun!
Thurs. and Fri., 8 p.m.; Sat. 2 p.m. and 8 p.m. Adults $15; children under 12 $8.00; senior citizens and college students $5.00. 555-9304.

The **Hester Street Cinema,** at 24 Hester Street, offers classic and arts films in a refurbished 1920 theater. During intermission, patrons are entertained with newsreels from the '30s and '40s and a player piano.
Shows are at 2, 5, and 8 p.m., with an additional show at 11 a.m. on weekends.

10

JOB 5 (page11 of 18)

CHILDREN'S ATTRACTIONS

Families will find plenty to do in Glover to keep children happy. At **Pickett Park** and **Lighthouse Beach**, children can swim (lifeguards are always on duty), play in the sand or on the playground, and collect shells from our well-tended beaches. **Glover Commons** features another playground for children's use. **The Glover Museum** offers many hands-on, child-friendly exhibits. In addition, Glover offers the following children's attractions:

Elder Farm has been a working family farm since the early 1800s. Children are invited to join in the work and fun. Milking a goat, sowing seed, riding in a hay wagon, collecting eggs, and feeding the animals are only some of the "chores" Farmer Joe and Farmer Becky give their little farmers. Tours last for two hours. Reservations a day or so in advance are recommended, particularly in the summertime.
1 Orchard Lane. Mon. - Sat., 9 a.m. - 5 p.m.; Sun. 11 a.m. - 5 p.m. 555-4007.

Place Photo K here.

Four Star Lanes offers candlepin bowling for little bowlers. Arcade games and a refreshment stand make for an evening of family entertainment.
40 Bridge Street. Mon. - Sat., 11 a.m. - 11 p.m. 555-0195.

A working miniature steam engine with tiny cars for children to ride, **Glover Railroad** takes its passengers on a 1-mile tour around Fairy Tale Land, complete with a treat from Mother Hubbard's cupboard. A carousel and petting zoo round out the fun.
8 Pine Street. Mon. - Sun., 9 a.m. - 5 p.m..

At **Pelican Miniature Golf,** children have their own special clubs for completing 18 holes of fun, including dinosaurs, a covered bridge, a cave, and a miniature raceway. An adjacent playground and ice cream store round out an afternoon of enjoyment.
24 Ossoff Street. Mon. - Sat., 11 a.m. - 5 p.m.; Sun. 1 p.m. - 6 p.m. 555-1993.

No visit to Glover is complete without a stop at **White's Penny Candy Store.** Strategically located near several schools, White's is perhaps the only

11

JOB 5 (page 12 of 18)

store left in the country that truly offers candy for a penny. Children can choose from old-fashioned and regional favorites such as licorice whips, root beer barrels, rock candy, maple sugar candy, and saltwater taffy.

32 Cabot Street. Mon. - Fri., 1 p.m. - 7 p.m.; Sat. 9 a.m. - 5 p.m. 555-1570.

ACCOMMODATIONS

Glover offers visitors a fine old hotel, two well-rated motels, and several bed-and-breakfasts for overnight stays.

The Cabot Hotel, at 5 Cabot Street (555-0680), built in 1814 and in continuous operation since that time, offers single and double rooms and suites, furnished with period reproductions. The hotel is within walking distance of shopping and historic sites. Its restaurant serves seasonal New England cuisine for every meal as well as a Sunday brunch and afternoon tea. The hotel has banquet facilities for up to 250 people.

The Briarley Guest House, at 3 Briarley Lane (555-5503), is a French Second Empire-style home meticulously restored and furnished with Victorian antiques and reproductions. The house has nine rooms with private baths, some with fireplaces. The Guest House offers private parking and a complimentary continental breakfast.

Place Photo L here.

The Dane Street Inn, at 12 Dane Street (555-5503), offers ten beautifully appointed rooms with private baths in a carefully restored 1843 home with Greek Revival architecture. Enjoy a gourmet breakfast and a view of the sea. The Dane Street Inn was rated best on Cape Ann by the *Boston Courier.*

The **Fawley Motor Lodge,** at 84 Bridge Street (555-6800), offers motel units, efficiencies, stoves, refrigerators, wall-to-wall carpet, air conditioning, color TV, and cable. The Lodge is located near restaurants, downtown, beaches, and train service to Boston. Weekly rates are available.

Hancock House, at 37 Beach Street (555-9427), is a fine old Colonial home overlooking the sea. Built in 1793 by a Glover merchant, the house features seven well-appointed single and double rooms—three with views of the sea—and two shared baths. A continental breakfast is offered. Reservations are recommended.

12

JOB 5 (page 13 of 18)

Travelers Haven, at 14 Peabody Street (555-6800), offers 120 comfortable guest rooms with cable, an indoor pool, air conditioning, and a restaurant on the premises. Minutes from downtown Glover and the beaches.

RESTAURANTS

Glover's conveniently located restaurants offer food for every taste and budget.

Annie's Corner Cafe serves lunch and dinner in a comfortable and quietly elegant atmosphere. The lunch and dinner menu features a variety of gourmet pizzas and sandwiches as well as pasta dishes, fresh fish, and chicken. Several vegetarian entrees are offered.
13 Front Street. Mon.-Sun., 11 a.m. - 10 p.m. 555-1692.

Local folks know that **the Clam Shell** is the place for fresh and tasty fried clams, lobster rolls, steamers, french fries, and onion rings. Try their home-made birch beer, a local favorite, akin to root beer.
6 Bridge Street. Mon.-Sun., 11:30 a.m. - 10:30 p.m. 555-1129.

For a fine seafood meal in an elegant atmosphere, try **the Clipper.** Favorite fare includes clam chowder, baked scrod, Cape Ann codfish pie, baked herb-stuffed clams, Falmouth codfish with shrimp, and cod steak in lemon and hazelnut sauce.
6 Ossoff Street. Mon.-Sun., 4 p.m. - 11 p.m. 555-3259.

Place Photo M here.

The Common House, rated best Sunday brunch in town by the *Glover Times,* offers hearty meals of seafood and steaks in a restored 1820 tavern.
11 Rantoul Street. Mon.-Sun., 11 a.m. - 11 p.m.. 555-8753.

The Depot Coffee Shop offers gourmet coffee, fresh-brewed tea, homemade doughnuts, strudel, and other delights.
94 Bridge Street, at the train station. Mon.-Sun., 6 a.m. - 11 p.m. 555-1240.

Glover Kitchen offers casual family dining with a nautical theme.
8 Cotter Street. Mon.-Sat., 8 a.m. - 8 p.m. 555-8836.

13

For notes on solutions, see page 132.

GLOVER, MASSACHUSETTS, VISITORS BUREAU (SIMULATION): SAMPLE SOLUTIONS

JOB 5 (page 14 of 18)

With 18 different varieties of pancakes on the menu, as well as homemade blueberry, cranberry, and apple muffins, **Hoppy's Pancake House** is a bustling place at breakfast-time. For hearty appetites, Hoppy's offers its famous Eight-Cake Stack.
24 Bridge Street. Mon.-Sat., 11 a.m. - 11 p.m.; Sun., 11 a.m. - 5 p.m. 555-1550.

Lena's Ice Cream "By-the-beach" sells homemade ice cream in 25 flavors. Sundaes, banana splits, milkshakes, and frappes round out the menu.
9 Dane Street. Mon.-Sun., 11 a.m. - 11 p.m. 555-8512.

Pinciaro's offers perhaps the best pizza in an area noted for good Italian food, as well as antipasto, chicken toscana, scampi linguine, lasagne, and fettucine. Try the house special, Pinciaro's Cheese Topper, with three kinds of cheese and a generous helping of Pinciaro's secret sauce.
18 Hester Street. Mon.-Sat., 11 a.m. - 11 p.m. 555-2525.

Place Photo N here.

At **Soup and Salad Express,** there's always room for one more trip to the magnificent soup and salad bar, with three homemade soups offered daily, and fruit and yogurt for dessert.
10 Front Street. Mon.-Sun., 11:30 a.m. - 9:30 p.m. 555-7450.

Super Sub offers great submarine sandwiches, fresh-made cole slaw and potato salad, steak fries, and onion rings. Home of the Super Sub, 12 feet of gustatory indulgence. Bread and rolls are baked on the premises.
16 Dane Street. Mon.-Sun., 11 a.m. - 11 p.m. 555-3082.

Place Photo O here.

14

JOB 5 (page 15 of 18)

Glover Summer Calendar of Events

Glover offers you a summer of free music under the stars, festivals, a treasure hunt, and fun! For details about any of these events, call 555-2000.

June 6-8
BAND SHELL CONCERT AT PICKETT PARK
An evening of Mozart by the Glover Community Orchestra. 6 p.m. - 8 p.m. Free.

Place Photo P here.

June 7-8
ARTS FESTIVAL AT GLOVER COMMON
One hundred New England artists, sculptors, and photographers will display and sell their work.

June 13-15
BAND SHELL CONCERT AT PICKETT PARK
The Marty Moreno Big Band brings you favorites of the Swing era. 6 p.m. - 8 p.m. Free.

June 14
CRAFTS FAIR AT CITY GARDENS
Fifty local crafters offer their wares. 9:30 a.m. - 9:30 p.m. Free.

June 20-22
BAND SHELL CONCERT AT PICKETT PARK
Resolution plays its innovative jazz compositions. 6 p.m. - 8 p.m. Free.

June 21
ICE CREAM SOCIAL AT GLOVER COMMON
Entertainment will be by the Wickersham Barbershop Quartet.

June 27-29
BAND SHELL CONCERT AT PICKETT PARK
The Govan Quartet entertains with Celtic music. 6 p.m. - 8 p.m. Free.

15

JOB 5 (page 16 of 18)

June 28
GLOVER AWARENESS DAY
Coordinated volunteer effort to clean up the city and help our neighbors. Free food and T-shirts. Come join in the fun! 9 a.m. - ?

July 4-6
HERITAGE DAYS IN GLOVER
Parade, midway, reproduction of Glover village, patriotic music, fireworks, and more! Call 555-2000 for details.

July 10-13, July 17-20
THE CARNEVALE CARNIVAL AT PICKETT PARK
This well-loved carnival comes to town every year with favorite rides, well-cared-for animals, and a wonderful arcade. Don't miss it! 4 p.m. - 11 p.m.

July 11-13
BAND SHELL CONCERT AT PICKETT PARK
The Narragansett Pops play show tunes. 6 p.m. - 8 p.m. Free.

July 12
CAPE ANN FLOWER COMPETITION AT BROUGHTON GARDENS
Open to all Cape Ann residents.
10 a.m. - 5 p.m. $1.

July 18-20
BAND SHELL CONCERT AT PICKETT PARK
The Glover Community Orchestra plays Bach. 6 p.m. - 8 p.m. Free.

July 19
TREASURE HUNT AT LIGHTHOUSE BEACH
For children ages 6-12. Pirate Patty and her talking parrot, Max, lead children on a treasure hunt where every buccaneer is guaranteed to find a doubloon or two. Free.

July 25-28
BAND SHELL CONCERT AT PICKETT PARK
Get ready for rock and roll with the Getters! 6 p.m. - 8 p.m. Free.

16

JOB 5 (page 17 of 18)

July 26
SEAFOOD FESTIVAL AT THE SEA WALL
Sample the finest seafood creations of Glover's restaurants. Crafts, storytelling, musicians, and more.

Place Photo Q here.

August 1-3
BAND SHELL CONCERT AT PICKETT PARK
Andy Albright and friends play the blues. 6 p.m. - 8 p.m. Free.

August 2
MAGIC BY THE GREAT BARBERESI AT THE GLOVER MUSEUM
Enjoy the lighthearted magic of this popular local magician. 2 p.m. $4.00.

August 8-10
BAND SHELL CONCERT AT PICKETT PARK
The Marty Moreno Big Band returns for three evenings of swing. 6 p.m. - 8 p.m. Free.

August 9
BEACH BLANKET PARTY
Join the Getters for a cookout by the beach, and dance to classic rock and roll. Sunset - 10 p.m. Free.

August 15-17
BAND SHELL CONCERT AT PICKETT PARK
The Glover Community Orchestra offers a special concert of children's favorites. 6 p.m. - 8 p.m. Free.

August 16
GREAT SCHOONER RACE AT THE SEA WALL
Come and cheer your favorite on as 100-ft. schooners race for the coveted Glover Cup! Before the race, enjoy the parade of sails and other maritime activities. 10 a.m. - 7 p.m. Free.

August 22-24
BAND SHELL CONCERT AT PICKETT PARK
Enjoy the music of Gilbert and Sullivan with the Glover Opera Company. 6 p.m. - 8 p.m. Free.

17

JOB 5 (page 18 of 18)

August 22-31
GLOVER FAIR AT THE FAIRGROUNDS, 1 DANA STREET
Exhibits of livestock, produce, plants, and crafts, along with food,
entertainment, and midway fun. 10 a.m. - 11 p.m. daily. Adults $4.50;
children under 12 $2.00; children under 5 free.

August 23
GLOVER MARATHON
This will be the 18th year for this 10K race, which begins at Glover Common
and proceeds through the downtown area, along Planter's Path, and through
the town. Music, food, raffles, and prizes. Proceeds to benefit the American
Heart Association. 7 p.m.

August 29-31
BAND SHELL CONCERT AT PICKETT PARK
Sit back for an evening of enjoyment with the Wickersham Barbershop
Quartet. 6 p.m. - 8 p.m. Free.

August 30
HARVEST FESTIVAL AT ELDER FARM
Fresh-pressed cider, apple-bobbing and a taffy pull for youngsters, folk art
exhibit and sale, music, hot-air balloon rides, and more!

18

JOB 6 (page 1 of 2)

The Glover Visitors Bureau

14 Cabot Street
Glover, MA 01915-4459
(508) 555-2000

Thank you for your recent visit to Glover. We hope you enjoyed your stay.

We value your opinion. So that we may serve you better, please fill out this survey and
return it in the enclosed postage-paid envelope.

1. If you took a Visitors Bureau tour, which tour did you take?

☐ Morning Walkers Tour ☐ Afternoon Walkers Tour
☐ Weekend Walkers Tour ☐ Senior Citizens Bus Tour
☐ Garden Bus Tour ☐ Family Bus Tour

Did you like your tour? ☐ Yes ☐ No

If you answered *No,* what about your tour didn't you like?

_____
_____
_____
_____

Do you have any suggestions for additions to our tours, deletions from our tours, or
other types of tours?

_____
_____
_____
_____

2. Which of the following attractions did you see?

☐ Foxx House ☐ Abbott Gardens
☐ First Baptist Church ☐ Bancroft House
☐ sea wall ☐ Nathaniel Westcott's House
☐ Pickett Park ☐ City Gardens
☐ Moriah Arboretum ☐ Broughton Gardens
☐ Olde Meeting House ☐ Glover Common
☐ Lighthouse Beach ☐ Glover Museum

Please give us your comments on any of these attractions.

_____

You have more space to write on the other side of the page.

JOB 6 (page 2 of 2)

2

_____
_____

3. What else did you see in Glover that you particularly enjoyed or disliked? Why?

_____
_____

4. If you stayed overnight in Glover, where did you stay? Please add any comments on your accommodations.

_____
_____
_____

5. If you did any shopping in Glover, how did you like your shopping experience?

_____
_____
_____

6. How were our restaurants?

_____
_____
_____

7. Was the Visitors Bureau helpful, or not helpful? In what way?

_____
_____
_____

8. Would you consider coming back? Why or why not?

_____
_____
_____

Thank you for taking the time to fill out this survey.

JOB 7

**Closings and Advisories
at Oceans, Bays, and Beaches**

There were **3,522** closings in 1995.

Closings were up **50%** from 1994's figures.

Disease-carrying organisms, mostly from
stormwater runoff and sewage overflows,
caused the closings.

▲ ▲ ▲

National Resources Defense Council. From *Testing the Waters VI: Who Knows
What You're Getting Into,* July 1996. "Beach Closings Up 50%." NRDC Reference
Online. Working Assets Online. 11 November 1996.

For notes on solutions, see page 132.

GLOVER, MASSACHUSETTS, VISITORS BUREAU (SIMULATION):   SAMPLE SOLUTIONS

JOB 8

INDEX

ATTRACTIONS

Pinciaro's
Soup and Salad Express
Super Sub

Abbott Gardens 8
Bancroft House 7
Broughton Gardens 10
Elder Farm 11
Four Star Lanes 11
The First Baptist Church 6
The Foxx House 6
Glover Common 6
The Glover Museum 8-9
The Glover Opera Company 10
Glover Railroad 11
Glover Trail 6-9
The Hester Street Cinema 10
Lighthouse Beach 9-10
Moriah Arboretum 10
Nathaniel Westcott House 9
The Olde Meeting House 6
Pelican Miniature Golf 11
Pickett Park 9-10
Planter's Path 9
The sea wall 9
White's Penny Candy Store 11-12

RESTAURANTS   13-14

Annie's Corner Cafe
The Clam Shelll
The Clipper
The Common House
The Depot Coffee Shop
Glover Kitchen
Lena's Ice Cream

SHOPPING   4-7

Amity Pottery
An Idle Hour
Cabot Cottage
Findlay Fruit and Vegetable Market
Glover Museum Gift Shop
Gordon's Department Store
Hannah Sisters Florists
Kingdom Toys
Laurie's Antiques
The Magic Carpet
Marvel's Pharmacy
Metamorphosis
The Minuteman
Pride's Pantry
Ron's Factory Outlet
The Ryder Bike Shop
Wyman's Yarn and Craft Shoppe

ACCOMMODATIONS   12-13

The Briarley Guest House
The Cabot Hotel
The Dane Street Inn
The Fawley Motor Lodge
Hancock House
Travelers Haven

**SUMMER CALENDAR
OF EVENTS   15-18**

$1.00 OFF   GLOVERS VISITORS BUREAU TOURS

This coupon entitles bearer to a $1 discount per person on any
Visitors Bureau Tour.

Expires September 8, 19--

Students are given very little direction on how to complete these projects; thus, solutions will vary widely. All documents should be 8.5" by 11" except where otherwise noted. In Jobs 1 and 2, the newsletter should be 4 pages and should have a volume and issue number, the Bureau name and address (shown on page 233) in the masthead, and the student's and supervisor's name and title (see page 232). The newsletter should have a half-page mailing panel roughly matching that of the example, with the permit number 7580. The Job 1 template should include set locations for Band Shell Banter," "Bed-and-Breakfast News," and "The Itinerant Gourmet," and a movie review. In Job 2, the issue date should be June 1-15. Ad sizes should match those in the example (see the template file ADCOPY for a list of ad sizes). The content of the "Band Shell Banter" article will vary, since students will write it, but data should match those in example. Students should have caught planted spelling errors in template disk files for Job 2. Job 3 should include the information shown. Job 4 should be 2 pages, 3 panels per page, and should include the text shown. The text of the brochure should begin on page 2 as shown; the center and right panels on page 1 should include the information shown in the example. The Visitors Bureau address information, particularly the phone number, should be in large type. Job 5 should be 5.25" by 8.5". The choice of photos and where to place them will vary widely. The document should include one spot color, applied appropriately. Text should be as shown throughout, except for the write-ups of Marcel's Pharmacy, the Magic Carpet, Gordon's, Findlay's Fruit and Vegetable Market, the Ryder Bike Shop, the Depot Coffee Shop, Hancock House, the June 5-8 and June 13-15 band shell concerts, and Heritage Days, which students will develop from the Job 2 newsletter. Students should also prepare a photo key document that lists each photo and reminds the printer of the final page size and to remove the photo boxes and statements. In Job 6, the wording of questions will vary; students may have added questions. For Job 7, students should have created two or three presentation graphics based on research on beachwater pollution—Internet research if they had access to the Internet, library research if they did not. Each graphic should have a complete source citation. Students should also provide copies of the articles on which their graphics are based. Job 8 should be 5.25" by 8.5". Text content should be the same as in the example.

APPENDIX A: USING A MOUSE

EXERCISE 1A

DISK FILES: Any file that contains text

LEVEL: 1

LEARNING OBJECTIVE:

Perform basic mouse actions

TERMS: mouse, point, click, double-click, drag

PREPARATION/MATERIALS:

Students will need to be in a program that uses a mouse and allows text selection. A word processor would be best, but students can also use their desktop publishing program.

TEACHING SUGGESTIONS:

- This exercise is intended for students who have never used a mouse or who need to practice their mouse skills. Ideally, it should be completed before students do Exercise 1. Students who are proficient with a mouse should skip this exercise.

- You may need to help students start their software and open their file.

- Demonstrate holding the mouse and moving it on the work surface. Note the corresponding movement of the pointer.

- Demonstrate some of the different forms the pointer assumes for different tasks.

- Define or review the following terms while demonstrating common actions, such as opening menus or selecting text:

Point	Move the mouse so that the pointer points to an item.
Click	Tap the mouse button once quickly.
Double-click	Rapidly tap the mouse button twice.
Drag	While holding down the left mouse button, move the mouse to another location.

- You may need to assist students in closing their document without saving it.

SETTINGS:

Not applicable.

SOLUTION:

Not applicable.

EXERCISE 2A

FILENAME: —

LEVEL: 1

LEARNING OBJECTIVES:

Select menu items
Select dialog box items

TERMS:

menu, menu bar, dialog box (pop-up box)

TEACHING SUGGESTIONS:

- This exercise is intended for students who have never used menus or dialog boxes or who need to refresh their skills. Ideally, it should be completed before students do Exercise 1. Students who are comfortable using menus and dialog boxes should skip this exercise.

- This exercise assumes that students are already in their desktop publishing program. You may need to help them start the program.

- Show students the menu bar on their software. Instruct them on the method(s) of opening and closing menus in their software. Have students practice opening and closing menus.

- Menu commands in desktop publishing software may have check marks, arrows, keyboard shortcuts, ellipses, or other markings; some options may be gray. Have students open appropriate menus so that they can see examples of each such treatment. Explain the meaning of each. Where appropriate, have students select menu commands.

- Have students select a command that opens a dialog or pop-up box. Have them make selections in the dialog box they have opened. Tell them how to exit from the dialog box without executing the changes they have made.

SETTINGS:

Not applicable.

SOLUTION:

Not applicable.

APPENDIX A: WORKING WITH WINDOWS

EXERCISE 3A

DISK FILES: —

LEVEL: 1

LEARNING OBJECTIVES:

Work with windows

TERMS: window, title bar, close box, maximize (zoom) box, minimize box, size box, scroll bars, scroll bar arrow, scroll box, icons, folders, program groups

PREPARATION/MATERIALS:

Consider making copies of the transparency on the next page, or of a screen dump from your software showing a typical window, for students' use.

TEACHING SUGGESTIONS:

- This exercise is intended for students who have never worked with windows or who need to practice their windows skills. Ideally, it should be completed before students do Exercise 1. Students who are proficient with windows should skip this exercise.

- You may need to help students open a window and an application.

- Show the transparency on the next page or a screen dump from classroom software if you have prepared one. Identify each part of a window, referring to the information on page 242. Discuss any differences between the window students have opened in their software and the window in the transparency.

- Demonstrate how to click on scroll bars and scroll bar arrows to change the view of the screen. Show how to drag a scroll box to move a precise distance.

- Have students identify several different types of icons.

- Demonstrate how to re-size windows in classroom software. Show students how to restore windows to their size before re-sizing. If your software has options for arranging windows (e.g., Cascade), demonstrate these as well.

- Show students how to switch between and move windows.

- You may need to assist students in closing their windows.

SETTINGS:

Not applicable.

SOLUTION:

Not applicable.

The PageMaker 6.0 Windows Publication Window

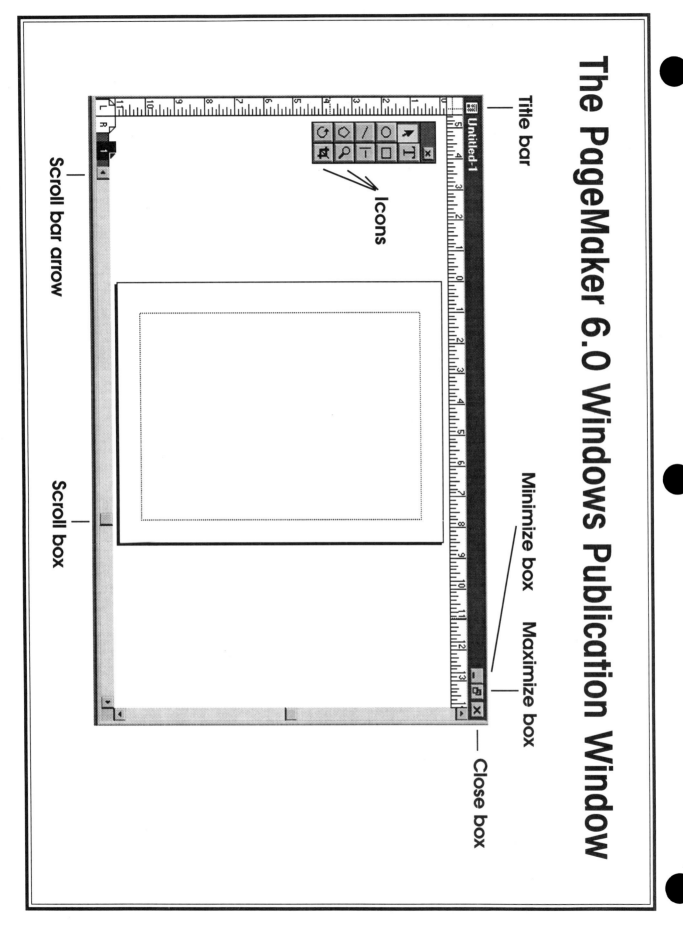

Title bar

Icons

Scroll bar arrow

Scroll box

Minimize box

Maximize box

Close box